A Lady's Captivity
Among Chinese Pirates

A Lady's Captivity *Among* Chinese Pirates

in the Chinese Seas

by Fanny Loviot

with an introduction
by Margarette Lincoln

NATIONAL
MARITIME
MUSEUM

Original spelling, grammar and capitalization retained throughout.

Translated from the French of Mademoiselle Fanny Loviot
by Amelia B. Edwards

First published by
Geo. Routlege & Co., Farringdon Street;
and 18 Beekman Street, New York

This edition published by
the National Maritime Museum, Greenwich, London SE10 9NF
www.nmm.ac.uk/publishing

Introduction © 2008, National Maritime Museum, Greenwich, London

ISBN 978-1-906367-00-8

A CIP catalogue record for this book is available from the British
Library.

Printed and bound in England
by Cromwell Press Ltd, Trowbridge, Wiltshire

Mixed Sources
Product group from well-managed
forests and other controlled sources
www.fsc.org Cert no. TT-COC-2082
© 1996 Forest Stewardship Council
FSC

DEDICATION

MADAME AND FRIEND,

When I first related to you the following strange and eventful episode, you advised me, inexperienced as I was, to write and publish it. I had never written a book in my life; but you encouraged me to make the attempt. "Be simple," you said, "be natural, and even simplicity and nature will suffice to make your work attractive. Add nothing, and take nothing away. Relate all your sufferings, and bid your pen record the faithful dictates of your memory. You will at least find friends among that healthy class which loves the simple and the true. Leave geology and geography alone, and be only yourself – a young and courageous woman, cast into the midst of frightful dangers, and miraculously saved. Many as are the readers and writers of travels, few women have visited China, and none, save yourself, have such a tale of adventure to relate. Write, then, and fear nothing."

It was thus, Madame, that you persuaded me, and it is thus that I have obeyed you. I have lived, while writing, amid the scenes and sufferings of the past. I have once again experienced all the terrors of captivity – once again been tossed by tempests, blinded by incendiary flames, and threatened with uplifted sabres. Inasmuch as these things have moved me by the mere remembrance, so I trust they may interest others in the mere recital. They will at least bear the impress of emotion and truth.

I place myself, Madame, under your patronage, and beg that you will accept this expression of my respect and affection.

FANNY LOVIOT.

CONTENTS

INTRODUCTION

by Margarette Lincoln

In 1858 the French adventuress, Fanny Loviot, published this gripping account of her emigration to California during the Gold Rush and her horrific capture by Chinese pirates near Hong Kong. Few women had visited China; none had such a sensational tale to offer the avid readership for travel writing. Her book was an immediate success, rapidly translated, and published in London and Stockholm that same year. Loviot's original title was factual: *Les pirates chinois: ma captivité dans les mers de la Chine*. Her English translator, Amelia Blandford Edwards, titillated a

Victorian audience eager for stories of innocent females in distress, translating this as *A Lady's Captivity Among Chinese Pirates in the Chinese Seas*. But Fanny Loviot was no lady.

Loviot explains how, in 1852, she and her elder sister sailed for California in the aptly named schooner *L'indépendance* to engage in 'commercial matters' in San Francisco. The 'sister' is probably fabricated to add the respectability of a travel companion. Their avowed commercial interest disguises the fact that Loviot sailed from France by means of the Lottery of the Golden Ingots, set up in 1850 with the political motive of raising funds to remove indigents and undesirables on a one-way ticket to California. After 1851, when Louis-Napoléon Bonaparte seized dictatorial powers, it was particularly aimed at those with experience of bearing arms who mistrusted him. Between 1851 and 1853, France sent over 3,300 gold diggers to San Francisco in an almost exclusively masculine emigration.

Loviot writes for a broad audience and has an eye for interesting detail. She criticizes fashionable women in Rio de Janeiro, where the vessel stopped to re-provision, 'the amount of jewels worn by each would be enough to stock a shop window'. Rio's commercial drive seemed to exclude cultural pursuits, an imbalance signalled by the position of women in society: they were habitually lethargic, 'lounging nearly all day on sofas covered with matting, they disdain mere household matters'. Women received no education, could talk only of slaves and servants, and were cruel to both.

After fifteen days, *L'indépendance* sailed towards Cape Horn. Loviot endured 'all the miseries of a maritime journey': the loss of a sailor overboard, tempests, days of eating nothing but shark meat, sickness and boredom. After an epic, five-month voyage, she arrived in San Francisco and found lodgings in Montgomery Street, 'one of its handsomest thoroughfares'.

A central portion of the book is devoted to Loviot's colourful insights into this chaotic and violent period in Californian history. The discovery of gold in 1848 caused its population to soar from 14,000 to 300,000 in only six years. Vigilante groups, trying to maintain law and order, lynched as they saw fit. Loviot was particularly struck by the polyglot population in boomtown San Francisco, 'I was jostled every moment by the natives of eastern and western America, of Tahiti, of the Sandwich Isles, and of every part of the European continent.' Fresh provisions were scarce. The people who made fortunes were not those who mined but those who ran stores to support gold diggers, or those who sold liquor and ran gambling dens to fleece them of hard-won gold. Listed as a sewing-maid in the ship's passenger list, Loviot's intimate knowledge of these gambling houses suggests that like many single women in the town she worked as a prostitute.

After a year, she travelled to trade in Sacramento and other Californian towns, giving a vivid picture of harsh conditions. In Eureka, fifteen miles from Oregon, winters were severe: 'scarcely a day passed but I saw three or four frozen corpses brought into the town. As for our bread and meat, we had to cut it with an axe and hammer.' She wore male dress because in this 'savage and unsettled' country, she had a better chance of escaping danger unencumbered by skirts.

Loviot's account of different peoples reflects the distasteful racial prejudices of the time but her opportunities to compare behaviour slowly produces more balanced insights. Experience, for instance, forces her to examine received views of China and the Chinese. She describes Chinese hostility to foreigners, especially to women, but counterbalances this by praising the friendship of her fellow prisoner, Chinese merchant Than-Sing, who negotiated on her behalf with the pirates. On the fringes of society herself and conscious that France helped to secure American independence from Britain, she shows sympathy for African Americans oppressed 'in even this free land'. From the window of a stage-coach, she views bands of Native Americans, spurring across the plains and marvels at the contrast between 'savage and civilized life' but her account soon calls this contrast into question. She criticizes settlers and their impact on American Indians, 'driven from their hunting grounds, and forced to take refuge in the mountains'. Ultimately her sympathy and scepticism transcend colonialist attitudes.

After fire destroyed her business, on the invitation of another French tradeswoman she sails to Hong Kong, then under British rule. There she finds accommodation worse than in California, 'Everywhere, on the furniture, in the presses, hidden in your shoes, clinging to your curtains, and ensconced in your portmanteaux, you find spiders, beetles and mosquitoes.' Her descriptions of Chinese customs, and the life of Chinese Pirates at sea with their wives and children, resonate with the growing interest in Pacific Studies.

Captured by pirates, she is rescued against the odds. Admiral Sir William Hoste at Hong Kong put twenty-four marines at the disposal of her rescuers; P&O, which had operated a Far Eastern Service since 1845, lent this rescue team the paddle steamer *Lady Mary Wood*. Later she returned from Hong Kong to Paris by P&O's overland route via Singapore, Port Suez, and Alexandria. The strong British connection here helps to explain why the book was rapidly translated for readers accustomed to reports in *The Times* of successful British expeditions against Chinese pirates.

As Loviot describes her experiences, she constructs her identity as author. It emerges from the ambivalence of her position within the discourses of patriarchy, gender, class and colonialism. Attacked by pirates, for instance, she reverses the usual passivity of women in shipwreck literature, urging the crew to act to save themselves. The captain admonishes his crew, 'I blush to think that a woman should be braver than you!' Loviot roundly defied the mentality of an era that glorified female domesticity and, a forgotten heroine, richly deserves tribute today.

Further Reading

Madeleine Bourset, 'Une émigration insolite au XIXe siècle, les Soldats des barricades en Californie, 1848–1853', *L'Emigration française: études de cas: Algérie, Canada, Etats-Unis*, Université de Paris (Paris, 1985)

Cordingly, David, ed., *Pirates: Terror on the High Seas – from the Caribbean to the South China Sea* (Kansas City, 1996)

Malcolm J. Rohrbough, *Days of Gold: the California Gold Rush and the American Nation* (Berkeley, 1997)

CHAPTER I

IN the year 1852, on a fine spring morning, I arrived in Havre with my eldest sister, who was going, on commercial matters, to California. We spent several days in Havre; and on the 30th of May, being Whitsunday, we embarked on board the little French schooner called "Independence," the captain whereof engaged to touch at Rio for food and water. Besides the captain, the master, and the crew, our vessel carried eighteen passengers, all of whom were going to seek their fortunes in California. The weather was superb, and our captain took advantage of a favourable breeze to set sail. The quay was crowded with spectators, and it was not without some dismay that we overheard their observations on the size of our schooner. "Never," said they, "can such a boat double Cape Horn. The least puff of wind must swamp a nutshell like that!" It is easy to conceive the impression which opinions such as these were calculated to produce on two inexperienced *Parisiennes*, who, like my sister and myself, were travelling for the first time. We looked hesitatingly in each others faces; but it was too late. The time for hesitation was gone by.

In another moment we heard the captain cry, "Let go the moorings!" All was now over and the great sacrifice was accomplished. Farewell, dear friends – Farewell, France – Farewell, Paris, which is a fatherland within a fatherland! – Farewell, all that is comfortable – Farewell, fashion, amusement, peaceful sleep, home comforts – Farewell, in fact, to all that makes life pleasant! For five months, at the least, I must sleep in a hammock instead of a bed; the sky must be my ceiling, and the sea my floor. My only music will be the sound of the breaking waves, and the untaught songs of the sailors. We are going to seek our fortunes – to seek, but what to find? Leaning sorrowfully over the side of the vessel, my heart full of a thousand hopes and regrets,

I waved my handkerchief in token of farewell to the friends I left behind me. First the jetty receded; then Ingouville, with its amphitheatre of houses; Ste. Addresse, which owes its celebrity to Alphonse Karr; then Cape la Hêve; and then there remained only the sky and the ocean.

We spent seven days in the Channel – seven days of rain and fog, with a leaden sky above, and the angry waves below. I was very ill during this part of the voyage. Not till the Sunday, which was the seventh day after our departure, had I strength to venture upon deck. The beacon off the Lizard Point was just visible, and I stood there watching it, till the light finally disappeared.

The passage of the Bay of Biscay was accomplished, not without danger to our fragile bark. At length, after fifteen days on the sea, we came within the influence of a Brazilian climate. I was never weary of admiring those clear skies and glorious sunsets the beauty of which no art could adequately reproduce.

We were rapidly approaching Janeiro, when we were one day startled by a sound like the rolling of distant thunder. The sea was calm; there was not a cloud overhead, and no other ship in sight. The deck was crowded in an instant. The noise grew louder, and we gazed tremblingly in each others faces. The mate, who was on the look out, cried "Breakers ahead!" "Helm about!" replied the captain.

The order came just in time. Happily for us, our little schooner escaped with only a scratch.

Brief as this incident had been, the women were all either fainting or shrieking. As for me, I was petrified. I had not really understood the imminence of the danger; but I always looked upon the captain's face as a kind of sea-barometer, and, on this occasion, the barometer fell considerably. My poor sister was overwhelmed with terror. "Cheer up," said I. "You have been longing for an adventure ever since we started, and here is a promising commencement!"

Eight days after this we were in the roads of Rio Janeiro, and came in sight of the Sugar-loaf Mountain, which towers above the bay. I can hardly believe that there exists under heaven a more exquisite scene. It is ineffaceably engraved on my memory. I can still see those wooded hills, those solitary creeks, those delicious valleys, those trees which never know an autumn tint, that immense expanse of sea, and all that marvellous landscape, which, even as one looks upon it, seems more of a dream than a reality.

The entrance to the port is defended by several forts, amongst which are those of Santa Cruz, Villagagnon, and the Isle of Serpents. These two last, which are the most imposing, are built upon islands lying within the bay. At

Rio Janeiro we rejoiced to resume the manners and habits of Europe.

Rio is, as everyone knows, a purely commercial city. The harbour, the exchange, and the markets are crowded with merchants and sailors. The variety of costumes, the songs of the negro porters, the chiming of church bells, the diversity of languages and faces, German, French, and Italian, all contribute to give a strange and lively aspect to the city.

During the fifteen days which we passed at Rio Janeiro, we visited all that was worth seeing in the city and its environs. The mountains, towards the north-east, are much built over. It is there that the Jesuit college, the Benedictine convent, the episcopal palace, and the Fort of Concéiado are situated. The architecture of these buildings appeared to me both heavy and ungraceful; but I much admired the aqueduct (finished in 1840), which brings the water from the torrents of Corcavado down to the city fountains. The imperial palace of St. Christopher is built at some distance from Rio, and is approached by a portico and a double colonnade. The promenade in front is planted with mangoes and laurels. There, like a true *Parisienne*, I did not fail closely to observe the *toilettes* of the Brazilian belles. Although these ladies profess themselves the devoted followers of our French fashions, they still indulge the Portuguese taste for ornament. The amount of jewels worn by each would be sufficient to stock a shop window; and they chiefly love to dazzle from a distance. On the whole, they are pretty; though perhaps a little too pale and sallow. With strangers they are familiar, perhaps even somewhat coquettish, and their nonchalance is particularly amusing. Lounging nearly all day on sofas covered with matting, they disdain mere household matters. As to their education, they never receive any; and their conversation is of the most uninteresting description. Their favourite topics are their slaves and their servants. It is no unusual sight to see these indolent women rouse themselves from their habitual lethargy, to run long needles into the arms or bosoms of the negresses who wait upon them. The society of Rio Janeiro is divided into *coteries.* The young Emperor of Brazil patronizes art, science, and letters; his people occupy themselves only with trade and money-getting. Indeed it is not long since a Parisian bookseller, of whom I enquired respecting the literature most in favour at Rio, replied that the books which sold best in the Brazils were those with red bindings! As to the commerce of Rio, it has increased of late to an enormous degree. Sugars, coffees, cottons, rum, tobacco, and other articles of native produce, are exported every year to the value of several millions of piastres. I can never forget the delight with which I visited the environs of Rio, or the delicious excursion that we made to the neighbourhood of Tijuca. It took us two days to get there; but we halted for the night at a piantation, where we were received with the utmost hospitality. Starting by daybreak the next morning, we proceeded through a labyrinth of delightful paths, and soon found ourselves face to face with the famous cascade, which is here precipitated into the midst of an amphitheatre of rocks. In the presence of this spectacle I must confess, in justice to myself, that I began to be somewhat consoled for the absence of Paris, and the Boulevard des Italiens. Often, O shade of Louis XIV! as I had seen the great fountains at Versailles, I now found them surpassed. Less agreeable, I admit, was the knowledge that these vast solitudes were peopled with jaguars and other ferocious beasts. After all, I prefer to admire wild animals in the Jardin des Plantes.

Having laid in fresh provisions, the captain took advantage of the fine weather, and we left Rio Janeiro. My sister and I had also stocked ourselves with good things; amongst the rest, with a large quantity of delicious little oranges, fine-skinned, perfumed, and sweet, which are sold in Rio for a mere song.

On the 7th of July we set sail once more for California. Seeing our little schooner depart on so long a voyage, the Brazilians proved themselves quite as discouraging as our evil prophets of Havre. "The 'Independence'," said they, "can never weather the tempests off Cape Horn!" My sister implored me not to continue our voyage; but, although I partook of all her fears, I remained inflexible. Independently of my desire to make a fortune, I felt myself impelled to go farther and farther away, and court the very dangers that I feared. I was proud of having crossed the line, and could not have borne to pause when half-way on the road. I had not much confidence in our schooner; but, had we chosen to go on by another vessel, we must have paid our fare twice over, and we had already spent as much as was consistent with our means.

Behold us, then, once more at sea, and, this time, for two or three months at the least. We talked, it is true, of touching at Lima, but on this head there was nothing certain. Our living was detestable; and despite the expostulations, and even the blows, with which our *chef* was stimulated, he never seemed to improve. My belief is, that he cooked entirely by chance. Wearied to death were we of potted meats, cabbage-soup, and half-boiled cod. These details are not poetical, but the facts are painfully true. On board the steamers (which put frequently into port, and carry cattle on board) the bill of fare is generally excellent; but in small merchant-vessels, such as the "Independence," the food is but too often scanty and unwholesome.

For a whole week we had the finest weather imaginable. There were five women on board; and we sewed, embroidered, and played *loto*, as cosily as in our own homes. Every evening we all assembled upon deck. There we talked and sang, and the singing, it is true, was not always very good; but at sea one's audience is not critical. Besides, it was pleasant to listen to French airs and choruses; and, when far away, all that recalls one's fatherland is welcome. By the way, I have forgotten to observe that our crew was entirely French.

And now the weather began to grow colder, and the sea, become more boisterous, no longer rocked us like a kindly nurse, but flung us rudely to and fro. Our embroidery, our *loto*, our singing came abruptly to an end, and we found ourselves subjected to all the miseries of a maritime journey. Every face was pinched, yellow, and discontented, and only groans and complaints were heard on every side. We were not absolutely in any kind of danger; but we were the victims of sickness and *ennui*. Thus several long weeks went by, and, day by day, the cold grew more severe. At length we came in sight of Cape Horn, clad in ice. Involuntarily, I thought of all the evil prophecies which had accompanied us since we started; but, to my great surprise, the nearer we approached the Cape, the more tranquil grew the sea. A dead calm ensued. For forty-eight hours we never stirred a foot. At length, towards the evening of the second day, the weather changed, the sea became agitated, and this time we found ourselves indeed menaced with one of those sudden storms which are peculiar to these latitudes. The captain instantly took in every sail. At this moment a young sailor was carried off the yards by a sudden squall, and was not missed until it was too late to save him. I can still hear the voice of the captain calling, and counting his sailors – "Jacques, Pierre, André, Remy, Christian, Robert, where are you?" "Here, sir!" "And Jean-Marie? Jean-Marie?" But Jean-Marie replied not. He had disappeared for ever, and of our eight sailors we had lost one. Poor Jean-Marie had been our ship's carpenter. It was his first voyage, and he was to have been married on his return. That night, all on board were sleepless. "They were right," thought I. "This Cape Horn is indeed a deadly and a dangerous spot!" The moaning sea and the sighing wind furnished a dreary accompaniment to these sombre thoughts. For twelve days we remained tossing to and fro without making any appreciable progress. On the thirteenth, we doubled the Cape. Soon after this, we sailed into a warmer latitude, and crossed the line for the second time.

And now the provisions became more and more scanty, wherefore we all complained bitterly of the shipowner. Eight or ten days more must, perforce, elapse before we could arrive at San Francisco; and, should we be delayed by contrary winds, it was just probable that we might die of hunger on the way. I began now to regret my own obstinacy, and wished that I had yielded to my sister's entreaties. While we were yet in this dilemma, our sailors caught a shark. It was so big, that, even after it was harpooned and hoisted on board, I dared not venture near it. Armed with their knives, our men speedily despatched it. It then was delivered over, piece by piece, into the hands of our abominable cook, who seasoned it with different sauces, and, horrible to relate, served it up for three successive days! We had, however, endured so many privations that every one pronounced it to be delicious, and only the captain and two sailors refused to eat it. Even they refused not from disgust, but superstition, believing that one day or other they might chance to be eaten in return.

If there be a delight unknown to those whose careless lives glide by in lettered leisure; if there be a joy untried by those Sybarites of great cities who seek to exhaust the pleasures of this world without risk or fatigue, it is that immense and ineffable rapture which overflows one's heart at the close of a long sea-voyage. Not till one has spent six months of life between the sea and the sky, the plaything of tempests, and subject to all the dangers of shipwreck and fire, is it possible to comprehend the intoxication of feeling with which one hears the sailor up aloft pronounce that magic word – "Land! land!" Everybody rushes on deck – the women burst into tears, for thus they translate every emotion of joy or sorrow – and the men, eager and triumphant, congratulate each other upon the distance and the dangers which are over at last. At sight of San Francisco, our passengers forgot all the sufferings of the journey, and began dreaming once again of the good fortune which awaited them. My sister and I followed the general example, and, for us, the present wore all the pleasant colours of the future. Poor France! thou wert soon forgotten, and we already opened our arms to this inhospitable land where gold is the only true God.

CHAPTER II

ON the 21st of November, 1852, we came in
sight of the little islands called the Farel-
lones, which lie at the mouth of the bay of San
Francisco, and of Bonetta Point, which, towards
the left, juts out to a considerable distance into the
sea. At this spot, a pilot came on board to conduct
our schooner through the narrow straits, which
hereabouts are scarcely more than half a mile

across. The steep rocks and sandy hills, all overgrown with brambles, which line the shore on every side next came into sight; and, immediately afterwards, a magnificent spectacle was presented to our view. We came, all at once, upon a fleet met together from every nation under heaven, as if to attest the importance of this modern city. Turning from the contemplation of these crowded masts, and parti-coloured flags, I beheld with surprise the scene of desolation presented by the sandy shores on the other side of the bay. There, all crowded together and falling to decay, lay the ruins of another fleet, scarcely less numerous than the first. Their faded flags hung in tatters from the broken masts; their decks had given way; and the moss was already growing in the interstices of the boards. They had long since been abandoned by their crews, all of whom, once landed, had fled away to the gold regions, and left their good ships to ruin and decay – melancholy examples of the greed of gain! Before the discovery of the gold mines, San Francisco was a harbour frequented by whalers, who put in there to refit and take in provisions. The dealings between the Indians and the European sailors were at that time limited to exchanges of skins. About half a century ago, a party of Spanish missionaries established themselves at some little distance from the coast, and built a small church called the Mission-Dolores, which exists to the present day.

When these Californian solitudes were overrun by Americans and Europeans in search of gold, that lonely spot, whither religious faith alone had penetrated, became one of the busiest haunts of San Francisco. A fine road was opened, buildings of all kinds sprang up around the modest chapel, and the road of the Mission-Dolores has now become one of the gayest promenades of the city.

At the time of my arrival (November, 1852), San Francisco presented a sufficiently curious aspect, with its sandy streets, it's planked footways, and its houses built of wood, iron, and brick. A marvellous activity prevailed in all parts of the city; and I was particularly struck with the coming and going of this polyglot population, composed of men and women of all races, complexions, and national costumes. I was jostled every moment by the natives of eastern and western America, of Tahiti, of the Sandwich Isles, and of every part of the European continent. Emigration had been going on very extensively for the three or four years preceding my arrival, and the population of San Francisco had consequently augmented to a total of something like sixty thousand souls.

But this city changes its aspect from day to day. Stone buildings were even then springing up in every direction. Montgomery Street, one of its handsomest thoroughfares, was paved, and bordered with superb buildings. Shops, warehouses, cafés, and magnificent hotels enlivened the street towards evening with thousands of lamps; and, seeing the crowds that issue at night from the Metropolitan Theatre, one can with difficulty believe that, only six years before, the Indians, lasso in hand, scoured this very spot in pursuit of the wild horse and the buffalo.

San Francisco had by this time become somewhat less expensive than formerly. It was possible to hire a furnished room for forty piastres per month, the value of a piastre being about four and twopence. This was considerably cheaper than the rents of many previous years, when shops were let at 100, 200, and sometimes 600 piastres per month. Meat and game were also much more reasonable. Mutton was sold at one piastre per pound, and veal at half a piastre. Milk, having at first cost one piastre the bottle, had fallen to two shillings, one shilling, and, finally, sixpence. Vegetables, on account of their scarcity, were sold at enormous prices. A pound of potatoes was not purchaseable at less than one shilling, and eggs cost from three to six piastres the dozen. The washing of a dozen articles of linen cost five piastres; a bottle of champagne, five piastres; and the cleaning of a pair of boots, two shillings. On the other hand, salmon was plentiful, and sold in all the markets at one piastre per pound. In the early days of San Francisco, one piastre would scarcely pay for the most simple repast without wine.

A great part of this population came originally from China; and if I first name these emigrants, it is because their colony, established in the midst of foreigners, presents many curious features. Their unsocial habits are already well known. Although their industrial inclinations drew them hither to this young fertile country, they nevertheless brought with them all the sullen and solitary instincts of their race. Thus, to avoid mingling with the Europeans, they congregated in a special quarter of the city. Sacramento Street, which is the centre of their colony, presents all the characteristics of a street in Canton, or any other Chinese city. Their commerce is exclusively confined to the products of their own country; and, in Dupont Street, they have gaming-tables always ready to tempt such of their countrymen as may be disposed to risk their hard-won gold.

An equally curious population may be found in another part of San Francisco. I allude to the blacks, who, like the Chinese, are settled altogether as one great family. They inhabit one entire side of Kearney Street; but the motives which have drawn them together arise from quite a different source. The Americans hate the negroes, and their antipathy is neither unknown nor dissembled. The contempt with which they are always treated, has, naturally enough, caused these latter to unite together in a quarter where they will neither trouble, nor be troubled by, their oppressors.

The reciprocal hate of these two races, the one so timid, and the other so arrogant, has induced between them a suspension of every social relation. The blacks are excluded from all public places frequented by their tyrants. They dare not show themselves at the cafés, the restaurants, or the theatres; and, having no other resource than dress, they parade the streets with cravats of the most dazzling colours, fingers loaded with rings, and dresses the delicate tints and textures of which contrast ridiculously with the ebon hue of the wearers. You chance, now and then, to meet a negro who is doing his best to imitate the manners of a gentleman; but he is sure to be absorbed in the perfection of his boots and gloves, and is altogether pervaded with an uneasy consciousness of his own dandyism. All the efforts of Mrs. Beecher Stowe have not yet availed to elevate the social position of the negro in the United States. The generous sympathy which this lady has manifested towards the coloured population appears simply ridiculous in the eyes of her own countrymen; and even in this free land, where the social rights of man have been at least conceded to them, the inferiority of their position is still so painfully apparent, that, after all, they can scarcely be said to have gained more than the mere privilege of making money and being their own masters.

The rest of the population consists chiefly of Americans, French, English, Germans, Dutch, Mexicans, Chileans, etc., etc.

Jackson Street is one of the most curious in San Francisco. On either side, the primitive wooden huts of the first settlers are still standing, and almost every dwelling is an eating-house, or "bar," as it is here generally called. After dark, when the gas is lighted, these establishments present a most extraordinary *coup d'œil*. The diggers, after a lucky day's labour, meet here for recreation; and this assemblage, gathered together from all parts of the world, makes up the strangest picture imaginable. The confusion of tongues and the variety of costume baffle description. Negresses, Mexicans, Peruvians, Chileans, and Chinese women decked out in furbelows and flounces, are seen hand in hand, and side by side with men who drink, and dance, and stamp, and shout for joy, to the sound of infernal music. Should you pause for a few moments before the door of one of these haunts, you are sure to witness some frightful quarrel, begun apparently in sport. This quarrel is but the lightning which precedes the thunder. The *melée* soon becomes general, and you had best escape while yet you may; for the quarter will be in commotion for the rest of the evening. Blood is sure to flow, and a formidable fight, in which many lives are sacrificed, but too frequently follows.

Still more curious is it to observe these people in the gaming-houses. There, by the light of glittering chandeliers, the contrast between these white, black, and bronzed faces becomes more startling than ever, crowded as they are around tables heaped with gold, silver, and ingots. When these gaming-houses were first started, and the gold-fever was at its height, many a serious fraças took place in the rooms, and, more than once, the winners found themselves paid with a pistol shot. It was then proposed to abolish the gaming-houses altogether; but, as the government exacted enormous rents for the hire of these establishments, they were eventually suffered to remain. The games are various. The Mexicans play chiefly at monti; the French at roulette, vingt-et-un, trente-et-quarante, and lansquenet; and the Americans at faro. I shall never forget the countenances of those professional gamblers who form, as it were, an essential part of these establishments. They are ready to play for others as well as for themselves, and there are few tables without three or four of these auxiliaries. Unruffled and business-like, they play on perpetually, and take no notice of whatever may be going forward. Playing for themselves, they win, on the average, from four to five dollars per diem; playing for others, they contrive to gain from eight to twelve. The windfall-gatherers are also deserving of mention. They are mostly Americans, who make it their business to pounce upon such stray coins, as are not immediately claimed by the winners. Watchful of every venture, they follow each turn of the cards, and, if a dollar be for one instant forgotten or left upon the table, an eager hand clutches and bears it off before the unsuspecting player has time even to recognize the thief. The proprietors of the gaming-houses favour these predatory individuals, and even help to distract the attention of the novice whom they have selected for their victim. This system of robbery is a sore trial to inexperienced players, and the consequences are often serious. The player who finds himself defrauded, scruples not to shoot the thief as if he were a dog. All these houses are provided with good orchestras, and the music sounds well to the chinking of the gold.

There is yet another and a more formidable class infesting these places. It is known by the name of the Black Band, and consists of a party of American swindlers. Well-dressed, skilful, and audacious, they follow their daring craft with utter impunity, and are the terror of the population. If they go into a gaming-house, it is with no idea of wasting their time on the chances of the cards. They find it more profitable and convenient simply to sweep off all the gold from the tables, after which they coolly walk away, and no one dares to stop them. These frauds are, as it were, consecrated by time and tradition. The police and the local government have as yet no power to put a stop to them, and, though the scandalous misdemeanours committed by the members of the Black Band would fill a volume, they are yet suffered to tyrannize over the entire community. Every day during my stay, some merchant's house was plundered, and did the loser dare to lodge a complaint against the robbers, they not only returned to the charge, but destroyed everything of value that came in their way. Nor was it all. They dined, drank, and helped themselves at all places of public resort, with the customary audacity; and, although their excesses had greatly diminished since the first peopling of the colony, there was not yet established, in 1852, any legal force sufficiently powerful to operate against them.

Arrived at San Francisco, we established ourselves in Montgomery Street, and hired a little furnished apartment, at a rent of three hundred francs per month. Considering that the walls were never dry, and that our bed was always soaked in rainy weather, we may be said to have paid somewhat dearly for our accommodation. We consoled ourselves, however, with the panorama which lay extended before our windows, and agreed that so glorious a prospect was cheap at any price; for it comprehended, not only the greater part of the city and the surrounding mountains, but included a bird's-eye view of the room in which the Committee of Vigilance had established its tribunal. This room was situated over a baker's shop, close under our windows, and a piece of cord attached to a pulley hung out from the first story, as an emblem of that simple and summary process known by the name of Lynch law. Not many days after our arrival, an execution took place. I chanced to awake very early that morning, and on opening my window saw two men busily occupied in fixing a new and unusually long cord to the pulley before mentioned. Already distant cries and the trampling of many feet announced something unusual, and in another moment the street was filled by an eager and angry crowd. I foresaw the terrible scene which was about to take place, and seized by an overwhelming terror, dragged my sister from the room, and left the house by a back door. In another quarter of an hour we were in the country, where we remained and spent the day with some friends. I afterwards ascertained that the criminal was a Spanish assassin. Arriving at the scaffold with a cigar in his mouth, he calmly addressed the crowd, and smoked till the very moment when the fatal noose was tied. The story that I had heard, and the sight that I had seen, left so painful an impression on my mind, that I was soon weary of my lodging in Montgomery Street, and hastened to seek another.

This terrible Lynch law is so called after an unfortunate man of that name, who became its first victim. The fatal and frequent errors which must necessarily ensue from this illegal system, may easily be conceived.

CHAPTER III

I spent a year at San Francisco, and, during that time, paid a visit to Sacramento, which is the second large city of California. The steamer took me there in a single day, and gave me an opportunity of admiring the river scenery. The city of Sacramento stands in the midst of a flat and fertile district, somewhat resembling the cultivated plains of France. The buildings, like those of San

Francisco, are built partly of wood, or brick, and partly of stone.

Here commerce is less active, and the heat more oppressive, than in the city I had just left. The surrounding marshes infect the air with pestilential vapours, and when the river overflows its banks, the country all around becomes one immense sheet of water. The gold diggers at one time poured by thousands into this unhealthy district; but the mortality amongst them was so rapid that, after the first brief harvest, they were glad to leave it.

For those who wish to go direct to Marysville by land, there is a comfortable stage-coach; but the roads are bad, and the jolting is terrible. When we had traversed about twenty miles of the road, we came upon Fort Sutter, which is inhabited by a tribe of Indians. Looking out from the windows of a stage-coach, and seeing these wild bands spurring across the plains, one is forcibly impressed by the contrast between savage and civilized life. Their complexion is tawny, their eyes large and black, and their expression, when not indicative of discontent, is innocent and wondering as that of a child. Their hair is straight and abundant, and black as jet, and grows down within half an inch of the eyebrows. Their dress consists of skins and quaintly-embroidered stuffs; on their necks and arms they wear an abundance of necklaces and bracelets, made of shells, glass-beads, and buttons. Notwithstanding all this finery, they are far from cleanly in their habits. They dwell in little dome-shaped huts, built up with clay and boughs of trees, and entered by a small opening near the ground. Here they crowd together, men, women, children, and dogs, and feed upon the produce of the chase and the river. Amongst other fish, they catch an abundance of fine salmon, which they dry for winter consumption.

These Indians never eat fresh meat; but, when it is putrid, either boil or grill it. They grow a kind of grain which they shell out into wooden bowls, work into a paste, and bake as bread. With this, they likewise eat grasshoppers and various other insects.

The traveller who pursues the road to Marysville, is tolerably certain to meet with more than one troop of aborigines. They have been driven into these desert regions before the advancing footsteps of civilization, and, although many of them, drawn thither by curiosity and that love of gain so common to all mankind, have ended by embracing the habits and occupations of the new comers, many others have, nevertheless, remained in open warfare, and several American expeditions have already been undertaken against them.

After eight hours of travelling, in the course of which we had forded several rivers, and encountered the worst roads I ever remember to have traversed, we arrived at Marysville.

With the exception of some few brick houses, Marysville is constructed entirely of wood. Situated on the enchanting banks of the Yuba, this city resembles an immense market-place, and does in fact supply all the villages and diggings round about. The heat here, however, is even more overwhelming, and the fever still more fatal, than at Sacramento.

It was in this city, and at the very hotel where I alighted in company with the rest of my stage-coach companions, that I met with an adventure which very nearly cost me my life. We were dining in company with a lady and her husband. Just as we had finished, and were about to leave the house, we heard an extraordinary commotion in the room overhead. The master of the hotel, in answer to our enquiries, replied that it was only a party of gentlemen who had met to dine upstairs. Being by this time tolerably well used to American manners, we were by no means surprised, but merely hastened our preparations, in order to get away before these revellers became more uproarious. It was a fine night, and we were anxious to pursue our journey by moonlight. Already the sound of broken plates and glasses foretold a serious ending to the riot. We waited to pay our bill, and suffered for our honesty. At the very moment when the master of the hotel was counting out our change, the door upstairs flew open, and the staircase was all at once filled by a drunken and vociferating crowd. We endeavoured to escape; but the fight had already begun. The combatants were all armed with revolvers, and in another instant I found myself separated from my companions. All at once a shot was fired, a ball whistled past my ear, and a second shot took effect upon a stranger who fell wounded at my feet. Distracted with fear, I ran I knew not whither, and was met by my friends, who believed me to have been injured, and were hastening to my help. The assassin, it seemed, had singled out a gentleman who ran for shelter down the passage where I was standing. Pursued and fired at, he nevertheless effected his escape; but the first shot passed within an inch of my head, and the second lodged in the left shoulder of an unoffending bystander.

The gloom of the passage, and the male attire which I habitually wore, had aided to mislead the would-be murderer. After all, I had a narrow escape of it.

It may not be out of place, at this point, to describe my costume, and to explain the motives by which I was led to adopt it. I wore a gray felt hat, a travelling paletot, and Hessian boots, such as were then the fashion in California. To these boots were attached a pair of Mexican spurs, useful for the mule-riding which is so frequent a mode of transit in these parts. Besides all this, I wore doeskin gloves, a leather belt made to carry gold, and a poignard. This dress is not only picturesque, but necessary; for the country is savage and unsettled, and, in moments of danger, the woman who is thus attired can better escape or defend herself than if she were encumbered with the garments peculiar to her sex. Up to the present moment I had never ceased congratulating myself on the success of my charming disguise; but this adventure, I must confess, somewhat diminished my confidence in my own temerity.

As may be conjectured by the preceding anecdote, the Americans, when intoxicated, are the maddest and most dangerous of human beings. They drink little wine; but, during their orgies, are much given to brandy, whisky, gin, absinthe, and other strong liquors. Their blood once inflamed, even the most peaceable among them become quarrelsome and sanguinary, and commit murders which, in their reasonable moments, inspire even themselves with horror.

Shasta City is a small settlement lying towards the north of California, and consists of a single street of wooden houses situated at some little distance from Sierra-Névada. This town was formerly the market which supplied certain rich diggings of the neighbourhood, long since exhausted. Instead, however, of being consequently deserted, Shasta City still flourishes in virtue of its situation. It is a halting-place for stage-coaches, and a station for the sale or hire of mules, without which it would be impossible to traverse the dangerous bridle-paths of the Rocky Mountains. Passing through this city, we beheld one of those great social disasters so common to California. Even at the moment of our arrival a great fire broke out, and in less than an hour the greater part of the city was consumed. Still more melancholy was it, towards evening, to see the unhappy inhabitants wandering amid the smoking ruins in search of the friends and fortunes they had lost.

Leaving Shasta City, and turning towards the north, as if bound for Oregon, the traveller passes through a mountainous country infested with enormous tawny bears, one of which alarmed me as I never wish to be alarmed again. I was riding somewhat in the rear of my companions. My mule was jogging slowly on, and, what with the fatigue of perpetual travelling, and the extreme heat of the day, I was more than half asleep. All at once, about twenty feet in advance, I beheld a huge bear peeping out at me from a cleft in the rocks, and swaying his head to and fro with the most tranquil and self-possessed air imaginable. The reins fell from my hands; the colour rushed to my face; I was paralyzed with terror, and had no voice to cry for help. The bear, however, content with the impression he had made, amused himself by rolling over and over in the middle of the road, without taking any notice of either me or my mule. A turn in the road now luckily brought me in sight of my companions. Their presence gave me courage, and, unwilling to prolong this exciting *tête-à-tête*, I put spurs to my mule, galloped rapidly on, and in another moment was indulging in a glowing description of the dangers through which I had passed.

Not far from Weaverville, where it was our intention to halt, we came upon Trinity River, on the banks of which many bloody battles have been fought between the Indians and Americans. Kneeling on the backs of our mules, we forded the stream, and landed among the rich pastures which clothe the table-lands all round about the city. Weaverville is the most northerly city of California, and lies amid a circle of mountains, the summits of which are covered with perpetual snow. Grouped together at the feet of these pine-clad mountains, the pretty wooden houses of Weaverville have a certain tranquil and pastoral effect, not unlike many an Alpine village. The air here is pure, fevers are unknown, and the whole place presents a delightful contrast to the unhealthy activity of San Francisco and Sacramento. The transport of letters and gold is carried on by an express postal service; and the auriferous riches of the district attract a considerable influx of visitors.

We sojourned for some time in this peaceful locality, which seemed as if it had never been visited by adversity or sorrow. Strolling one day in the outskirts of the town, I came upon a desolate-looking spot, in the midst of which stood two black crosses, such as are seen in the French cemeteries. They occupied the very spot upon which the foundations of a building were yet visible. Naturally curious, I hastened to enquire the history of these funereal emblems, and heard in reply the following narrative:

During the first or second year which followed the discovery of gold in California, there existed no form of regular government. Those miners, therefore, who first penetrated into the regions of Weaverville, were obliged, in a measure, to take the law into their own hands, and protect themselves and their property. Here they lived in a state of the most complete independence, subject to no taxation, and relying for safety upon their own courage and fire-arms. Soon the American Government recognized the necessity of organizing a political jurisdiction for the greater safety of those masses which were crowding, day by day, to the gold-fields of the new State. A system of taxation was forthwith imposed upon all the cities of California, and, amongst other measures, it was decreed that every digger should purchase the right of exercising his vocation. These new laws met, of course, with much opposition, and the sheriff who was despatched from San Francisco to Weaverville, found his office by no means safe or pleasant.

Amongst some of the first gold-seekers who penetrated to these mountainous districts, was an Irishman, who had here built his house, and established himself and family. Being summoned to open his door, in order that the sheriff might take an inventory of his goods, he declared himself ready to defend his domestic liberties with his life, and refused to admit any law-officer whatever, without some more convincing guarantee of his authority. Exasperated by this resistance, the sheriff, who was a man of savage temper and indomitable energy, and who had served in many an expedition against the Indians, replied only by a shot from his revolver. The unhappy gold-digger fell dead across the threshold of his door, and his wife, in trying to defend him, shared his fate. Henceforth, the new taxes were raised and paid without opposition. As for the Irishman's house, it was razed to the ground, and those two black crosses serve to perpetuate the spot where the victims were buried.

The greater proportion of Californian gold-diggers is Irish; and, at a distance of about three miles form Weaverville, there lies a little town called Sidney, which is exclusively colonized by these people.

During my stay in this district, I took advantage of an opportunity to visit some Indian prisoners, who had not long since been taken, and who were kept upon a piece of waste ground at some little distance from the city. Here they had built themselves huts, and dwelt as they might have dwelt in their native forests. They had been captured during an expedition which was lately undertaken to avenge the murder of an American merchant, and were here expiating the crimes of others. Amongst them was one man so old and decrepit, that it seemed as if he could scarcely live from one day to another. Turning slowly towards me, he uncovered his chest, and displayed a large and deep wound, from which the ball had not yet been extracted. Some few steps farther on lay a young Indian woman. A thick blanket was wrapped about the upper part of her body, and she wore a petticoat of fine matting, beyond which her lovely little feet alone were visible. Her wrist was broken by a pistol shot. Prostrate and motionless, she lay like a dead creature. Her face alone glowed with a kind of savage heroism, and her great black glittering eyes met mine steadily and coldly, as if she were insensible to pain.

Two savage dogs, of the species called *coyottes*, had followed the prisoners into captivity. These dogs live, like the Indians, in wild and wandering bands. They have short legs, smooth tan-coloured skins, and muzzles fringed like that of the fox. They abound in the desert country round about Oregon, and, unless impelled by hunger, rarely venture in the neighbourhood of the towns. Timid by nature, they fly at sight of man. Amongst the prisoners I observed several women, who were attending to their children, and cooking their food, after the manner of civilized nations. The men of these nomadic tribes leave all household matters to the women.

The children were playing happily together amid their sorrowful elders. The heads of two of the number had been lately shaved, in token of mourning. Their faces had also been blackened, according to the Indian custom, and I was told that their parents had been killed in the late attack. In this part of California it is only the women who are tattooed, and the men never shave their heads, excepting for the loss of a near relative.

We gave these Indian prisoners some game, a couple of gray squirrels, and three doves, all of which, in California, are accounted delicious dainties. Our offerings were received with good will, and the women, in return, presented us with some necklaces of shells.

Weaverville is the centre of a great mining district, and its commerce chiefly consists of provisions, household utensils, and tools used in the diggings. The land thereabouts is of a reddish hue and of a particularly auriferous quality. There are few spots which do not yield some profit to the pickaxe and cradle of the miner. Provided with these, he unearths and washes the nuggets. The first blow of the pickaxe, and the washing of the first cradleful furnishes him with an estimate of his harvest for the day; since he has only to measure his gains by the speed of his labour. It was attempted, at an immense cost of money and time, to turn the course of Trinity River, and convey a canal through the heart of the diggings; but the project was too gigantic, and the works were at length abandoned for want of capital.

The southern mines are much poorer than those of the north, and, consequently, enjoy a smaller share of popularity. There are two seasons favourable to the work; the one begins in November, during the rainy season, and the other after the melting of the winter snows in April or May. Were there more water in California, a larger amount of gold would be found, and the diggers would suffer fewer miseries during times of drought.

The profits of a gold-digger vary with the soil on which he works. Some gain five piastres per diem, others ten, twelve, and upwards. Some there are who, having chanced upon an unusually auriferous spot, make fortunes rapidly; but those of whom we hear nothing are the unlucky thousands, who, having abandoned their homes and families in the hope of gain, arrive too late, and find only those lands which have been exhausted by others. For such are these, despair and starvation alone remain.

A travelling gold-digger presents a somewhat eccentric appearance. He wears great leather boots, which reach considerably above his knees, a coarse woollen shirt, and a felt hat beaten out of shape. To the left of his belt hangs a bowie-knife, to the right a revolver. On his shoulder he carries his pickaxe, on his back his bedding, and round his neck his saucepan and his miner's cradle.

Leaving Weaverville for Eureka, which lies still farther to the north of California, we crossed a long chain of mountains, passable only by mules. We frequently rode beside abysses so frightful that we dared not look at them, and pursued sandy paths all seamed with serpent tracks. In the midst of these vast solitudes, we came now and then upon a party of muleteers. The tinkling music of the mule-bells, the crackling of the dry leaves under foot, and the mysterious vapours by which we were surrounded, all combined to add to the poetry of this strange and solemn scene. In a church I have often vainly striven to pray; but amid a nature such as this, prayer comes unbidden.

In consequence of the snow which had lately fallen, our journey was more than usually tedious and difficult. We frequently beheld the foot-tracks of the gray bear. Now and then we passed the carcasses of animals which had been devoured, and came, more than once, upon fresh blood-stains in the snow.

A few miles farther on, being quite overpowered by fatigue, we halted at a hut which had been built by some Americans, amid the regions of perpetual snow. We took them, at first, for brigands; but they were simply inn-keepers, who sold us cutlets of bear ham for their weight in gold. I had already tasted this dish at San Francisco, and found it on both occasions delicious.

In the heart of these Oregon mountains lie table-lands, which in summer are covered with the richest vegetation. They are, for the most part, cultivated by emigrants from the interior of the United States. The gathering together of these and other emigrant labourers, renders Eureka still more important as a place of business, than either Weaver-ville or Shasta City. It is a stopping-place, where travellers pause to lay in stores of provisions, and to make such purchases as are necessary for the pursuit of either mining or agriculture. In proportion, however, as the European and American population increased, it became more and more incumbent upon the Eurekans, to watch over their own personal safety. Driven from their hunting-grounds, and forced to take refuge in the mountains, the Indians cherished a profound hatred towards these new comers, and Eureka became the scene of a harassing nocturnal warfare. When I arrived at Eureka, the outrages which had lately taken place were the theme of every tongue. Whole farms had been burnt, and whole families massacred in the immediate neighbourhood of the city.

Eureka is but fifteen miles from Oregon, and we arrived there in the month of November, A.D. 1853.

The houses, and even the chief hotel, are here built of wood. As usual, wherever there are gold-diggings in the neighbourhood, there are gaming-houses in the city. At the restaurant *La Fayette*, which is the best conducted of these establishments, an excellent French dinner may be had. For all this, and despite the general tendency towards material comforts, it was difficult in 1853 to surround one's self with many of the luxuries of life. Everybody, for instance, slept upon straw beds, and mattresses were unknown.

The frosts this winter were so severe, that scarcely a day passed but I saw three or four frozen corpses brought into the town. As for our bread and meat, we had to cut it with an axe and hammer.

The mines of Eureka are also highly productive; but here, as elsewhere, the want of water is often sorely felt.

After staying in the city for twelve weeks, and having, by that time, disposed of our merchandise to considerable advantage, my sister and I returned to San Francisco. This fatiguing journey had tired us both severely, and we now entertained serious thoughts of establishing ourselves in business, and making our home in the city.

CHAPTER IV

AFTER eighteen months of Californian life, a
circumstance occurred, which changed, not
only my position, but my prospects. I became
acquainted with one Madame Nelson, a French
lady who, like myself, was engaged in commercial
speculations. It was, at this time, her intention to
leave California for Batavia, in the Island of Java,
whence she had already received many letters of

invitation, and where she believed herself certain of success. Being desirous that I should accompany her in this expedition, she proposed that we should travel together, and share the profits, as well as the fatigues of the enterprise. This matter was of too serious a nature to be hastily decided; but, while I was yet hesitating, an event took place which summarily decided it for me. One of those destructive fires so common in San Francisco broke out next door to us, in the dead calm of a lovely summer's night, and made such rapid progress that we with difficulty escaped. Startled from sleep, we had but time to collect a few valuables which we flung into a portmanteau, and threw out of the window. Scarcely had we gone twenty paces from the house, when staircases and flooring fell in with a tremendous crash. Three hours later, fifty-two houses were entirely destroyed. This fire cost us more than four thousand piastres, since we rescued nothing from our stock.

My sister, being utterly out of heart, made up her mind to return to Eureka, where commercial affairs were said to be unusually prosperous. As for me, I decided to accompany Madame Nelson; for, notwithstanding the pecuniary advantages which I hoped to derive from the journey, my love of novelty was in nowise abated.

We then drew up the following programme of our route:– Directing our course through the Chinese seas, we proposed touching at Canton, Macao, Hong-Kong, and Batavia, where we hoped to remain about two months. These matters settled, we had but to prepare for our departure.

On the 14th of June, 1854, we embarked on board the "Arcturus," bound for China. Our fellow-passengers consisted of four French artistes, going to Calcutta on a musical speculation. In addition to these, we carried thirty-five Chinese in the steerage.

On the fifteenth day of our voyage, we came in sight of the Sandwich Islands. My companion, who up to this time had proved herself an excellent sailor, became all at once languid and melancholy. Two of our Chinese passengers were professed fortune-tellers. Finding that they could both speak a little English, and hoping thereby to amuse Madame Nelson, I summoned them to an exhibition of their talent. Half laughing, half incredulous, my friend offered her hand to their scrutiny. Silently and sadly they looked at it, hesitated, and consulted together. Becoming impatient of this delay, Madame Nelson pressed them for an explanation. "We pause," said they, "because we fear to afflict you." "You are wrong," said she, "for I have no belief in your art." Annoyed, perhaps, by this observation, they framed an evil prophecy. "You have been wealthy," said they (and this was true), "but you seek in vain to accumulate fresh riches. Your days are numbered." Speaking thus, they gazed earnestly upon her, and seemed to read the future in the lines upon her brow.

Painfully impressed by this prediction, my friend yielded to a despondency which I tried in vain to dispel. I then regretted what I had done, and strove to conceal my uneasiness by consulting the necromancers on my own account. The second prophecy made up in a measure for the dreariness of the first. The markings of my hand, said they, were especially favourable. I was destined to prosperity, and should one day become rich. One of them then pointed to a line upon my forehead. "A great misfortune awaits you," said he; "but it will not affect your future prosperity." I only laughed at these predictions, and endeavoured to cheer my poor friend by every means in my power.

The next day she was more dispirited than ever. She contrived, however, to sketch the portraits of our Chinese soothsayers, with which they were much delighted.

Within eight days from this time the state of Madame Nelson's health had become truly alarming. We had no medical man on board, and my anxiety grew daily more and more insupportable. At length one of the Chinese offered to prescribe. In his own country he was a physician, and he proposed administering some pills, which, hitherto, he had never known to fail. These pills were red, and about the size of a pin's head. The French passengers agreed with me that it was better to trust the Chinese than leave Madame Nelson to die without help. We offered her six of the pills. She enquired whence they came, and we were so imprudent as to tell the truth, which immediately prejudiced her against them. Her resistance drove us almost to despair; and when she at length yielded, it was not from conviction, but in compliance with my entreaties. More than six, however, she would not take. Whether their number were too few, or administered too late, I know not; but henceforth she grew rapidly worse. A violent delirium seized her, during which she raved of the Chinese and their prophecies. The delirium was succeeded by spasmodic paroxysms. I bent sorrowfully over her; I drew her head to my bosom; and, seeing that death was close at hand, imprinted a farewell kiss upon her lips. She looked up, smiled languidly, as if to thank me for my love, and gently breathed her last.

That same night the sailors bore her body upon deck, and the captain read aloud the funeral service. This done, they wrapt her in a sheet, slung a cannon-ball to her feet, and consigned her to her grave in the deep sea. That sullen splash found an echo in the hearts of all present.

The death of Madame Nelson left me almost broken-hearted. Far from my friends and my country, I felt more than ever desolate, and lamented the fatal day which bore me from my native land. What was now to become of me, friendless and alone, in a strange and savage country? Alas! what would I not now have given to turn back; but I could not change the course of the ship, or turn the currents of the winds. Go on I must, and submit to my destiny.

The navigation of the Chinese seas is rendered more than commonly hazardous by reason of the sunken rocks which there abound. Threading these securely, we came, one glorious day, upon the Bashee Islands. In three days, said the captain, we should probably arrive at the end of our journey. Just, however, as we were congratulating our-selves on this pleasant intelligence, we were overtaken by a frightful storm of wind and rain. Huge black clouds tra-versed the sky, and we saw more than one water-spout in the distance. When the tempest at length abated, it was succeeded by a dreary calm, which lasted for nine days. A faint breeze occasionally sprang up, only to die away again, and leave us more impatient than ever. At length, after beating about the Chinese shores for more than twenty days, the captain informed us that our sea-stores were almost exhausted. Hereupon the sailors refused to work, unless some of their number were allowed to take a boat, and venture in search of Hong-Kong, which, we calculated, could not be distant more than thirty miles. The captain despatched eight men. We then cast anchor amid a group of islands, and there awaited the return of these brave fellows who had undertaken to risk their lives for our safety. Twenty-four hours after, they returned with a steamer, which towed us into the Hong-Kong roads, on the 29th of August, after a sea-voyage of seventy-six days. Summoned to the French Consulate to attest the death of my unhappy friend, I made the acquaintance of our vice-consul, M. Haskell, and explained to him all the discomfort of my present position. He advised me to relinquish an enterprise so unfortunately begun. I replied that my only desire was to get back to California. "Suffer me," said the vice-consul, "to make all the arrangements for your return; and I trust that my influence may be sufficient to ensure you every attention during the voyage." I thanked him for his kindness, and from this time became better reconciled to my Chinese expedition.

The island of Hong-Kong contains twenty thousand Chinese, and one thousand European inhabitants. It is situated at the foot of an immense mountain, and is built in the form of an amphitheatre. On entering the principal street, the traveller is surprised to find himself in the midst of elegant European buildings. The houses are very large, surrounded by verandahs, and fitted up with jalousies – a very necessary luxury in all tropical climates. On a height to the left of the harbour stands the town-hall, and, a little farther on, an immense line of barracks, for the accommodation of the English soldiery. In the midst of the parade, which is a kind of fortified esplanade, stand several pieces of cannon, so placed as to command the principal street of the town – an arrangement admirably calculated to ensure the respect and good conduct of the Chinese population. Here also is an English Protestant church. The climate of Hong-Kong is unhealthy. The summer heats are oppressive, and fevers are prevalent.

Life at Hong-Kong is monotonous to the last degree. Public amusements are unknown; society there is none to speak of; and it offers no resources beyond those of the domestic circle. The women never walk out. In the first place, it is not the fashion; and, in the second, it is scarcely possible, on account of the heat. Though it be to go no farther than the next house, you are always carried in a palanquin. The English gentlemen at Hong-Kong wear white suits, as in India.

Every kind of European trade is carried on at Hong-Kong for the benefit of the English residents. Few Chinese women perform any kind of manual labour; and, except in shops of the very poorest description, they are not even to be seen behind a counter. Costermongers and provision-vendors, peripatetic cake, fruit, and sweet-stuff sellers, and enterprising speculators in grilled fish, roast fowls, and other smoking delicacies, here abound. Of beggars, old and young, there is no scarcity; and the blind go about the streets ringing a little bell to attract public attention. Besides these, there are plenty of wandering singers and musicians, who recite quaint and monotonous legends "for a consideration."

Not the least curious members of the population are the barbers and hair-dressers, who twenty times a-day make the tour of the city, carrying their shaving apparatus on their backs. Should a shopkeeper or pedestrian wish to have his head shaved, his pig-tail dressed, or his eye-brows trimmed, he beckons to the first *artiste* who passes by, and the operation is forthwith performed, either in the shelter of a doorway, or in a shady angle of open street.

There are but two hotels in Hong-Kong, and both lodging and provisions are quite as expensive as in California. As might be expected, the accommodation is far inferior; and even the cleanest and best regulated houses are infested with frightful insects. Everywhere, on the furniture, in the presses, hidden in your shoes, clinging to your curtains, and ensconced in your portmanteaus, you find spiders, beetles, and mosquitoes. If you take out a garment for use, two or three of these disgusting creatures are sure to be lying in the folds of it. The beetles, however, are the most annoying of all; and at night, when the candles are lighted, become almost unendurable. One falls on your head; another alights upon your nose; and in the morning, when you wake, you are sure to find half-a-dozen lying drowned in your wash-hand basin, or served up, struggling, in your tea. At table you meet with them constantly in the gravy, or the vegetables; but this is a matter of course, and cannot be avoided.

The vegetation of Hong-Kong is the most luxuriant in the world, and the flowers are redolent with a perfume more sweet and more penetrating than those of Europe. Admitted to visit the garden of a mandarin, I scarcely knew which was the greater, my delight or my astonishment. It was an artificial world in little, interspersed with grottoes, rocks, rivulets, and miniature mountains. There was not a straight path in the place, and at each turn I came upon some fresh point of view. Here were fantastic kiosks with windows of coloured glass; rustic suspension bridges; and tranquil shrubberies, musical with birds. It is only in balmy solitudes such as these that the Chinese ladies can, with their pinched and mutilated feet, enjoy any kind of out-door recreation.

Taking advantage of the time that still remained to me, I agreed to join my fellow-travellers in a visit to Canton.

Just at this period the insurrection of 1854 was at its height, and, although the city itself was tolerably tranquil, the neighbourhood all around was up in arms. Under these circumstances, we could hardly hope to make any length-ened stay.

In this enormous city (only two streets of which were then accessible to Europeans), factories, English counting-houses, and extensive warehouses abound. There is not a single hotel in the place. At the houses where you wish to transact business, you send in your card. The retail dealers are classed as a separate body of tradesmen. One quarter of the city is wholly occupied by the porcelain-sellers, another by the tea-dealers, a third by the silk-merchants. I was never weary of admiring these magnificent warehouses, where are displayed specimens of the most exquisite handiwork imaginable. Lacquered furniture, ivory fans, carved jewel-cases, silken tapestries, and resplendent stuffs, distract the attention of the stranger at every step. The thoroughfare called New China Street is bordered by these superb stores, each of which has its flat roof decorated with parti-coloured balls, and its upright sign, where golden letters on a scarlet ground proclaim the name and trade of the merchant. The streets are filled by a busy, noisy crowd: strolling vendors, with their strange guttural cries; grave and solemn citizens, with their flowing robes and perpetual parasols; and, now and then, one or two women of the poorer class, hurrying along with children in their arms.

If a traveller desire to visit a Chinese interior, he will not be refused admittance to the houses of those merchants who are in the habit of trading with the English. Having sought and obtained the necessary invitation, I went one day to a house celebrated for its luxury, and belonging to one of the wealthiest mandarins of the city. I scarcely know how to describe what I there beheld. There were flowers, musical instruments, opium-pipes, and cigarettes. From the ceiling hung lanterns of every shape, colour, and material – lanterns in glass, gauze, and paper – lanterns fringed, tufted, hung with bells, and decorated in every possible manner. From the walls were suspended pictures representative of the very infancy of art, and varnished tablets inscribed with philosophical and poetical sentences. Above all, however, I was curious to visit the apartments of the women; but this was forbidden.

During the three days that I stayed at Canton, I witnessed a *fraças* amongst the Emperor's soldiers. A Chinese army is the most ludicrous affair imaginable. How shall I describe these absurd warriors, dignified by the titles of "War-tigers," and "Mountain-splitters?" Standing on a lofty terrace, I was quite near enough to distinguish all their proceedings. Armed with lances and cumbrous matchlocks, they crowded along in the greatest disorder, and almost every soldier carried an umbrella, a fan, and a lantern; all of which forcibly reminded me of the Chinese burlesques that I had seen in the theatres at San Francisco.

The perpetual thundering of cannon, the brawling and skirmishing of the insurgents, the frequent encounters which took place beyond the walls, and the false alarms by which we were continually harassed, all combined to hasten my return to Hong-Kong.

After I had been resident about a month in China, our vice-consul informed me that a ship was about to sail for California. He was so extremely kind as to interest the captain in my favour, and this officer, whose name was Rooney, promised to pay me every attention in his power. Having thanked M. Haskell for all the interest which he had taken in my affairs, I hastened to my hotel with a light heart, and prepared forthwith for my journey.

CHAPTER V

TOWARDS four o'clock in the afternoon, on the 4th of October, 1854, I went on board the brig "Caldera," which, under a Chilean flag, was about to set sail that evening for California. Such was the honesty and frankness of the captain's face, that I was immediately prepossessed in his favour. Mr. Rooney was a man of about thirty-five years of age, neither short nor tall, and, to all appearance, a thorough sailor. His countenance betokened an energetic character, and I would have staked my existence upon his courage and good nature. My first care was to visit my cabin, and arrange my luggage. Soon after this, we weighed anchor, and put out to sea. Once on the way, I was seized with a listless melancholy, for which I found it impossible to account. This melancholy, which might have been a presentiment, seemed all the stranger considering that I was returning to America, to my sister, and my friends. Resolved, somehow or other, to shake it off, I left my cabin and made the tour of the ship. It was a handsome three-masted brig of eight hundred tons burthen, well rigged, and gracefully built. I visited the saloon, the cabins, the captain's parlour, and another which belonged to the supercargo of a commercial house at San Francisco, the heads of which had a valuable cargo on board. The saloon was lighted from above, and elegantly fitted up with panellings of white and gold. So clean and orderly was every corner of the vessel, that it seemed as if nothing adverse could take place to interrupt our course; and I almost fancied that we might all be allowed to sleep away the three long months which must elapse before our arrival in California.

Of one of my fellow-travellers I shall often have occasion to speak. He was a Chinese of about fifty years of age, and an inhabitant of Canton. He had a commercial house at San Francisco, and was carrying with him a large stock of opium, sugar, and coffee. His name was Than-Sing. His features were of the type common to his nation, and deeply scarred by the small-pox. Though plain, however, he was not unprepossessing; for good-nature was expressed in every line of his countenance, and his smile was kindness itself.

We sat down four to dinner, and found that no two of us belonged to the same nation. The captain was English, the supercargo American, Than-Sing Chinese, and I French. I am thus particular in defining our several nationalities, in order to prove how much our difficulties must have been increased, in any case of peril, by the differences of language. Than-Sing spoke English as I did, that is to say, indifferently; but not one of the party spoke French. It will hereafter be seen how Than-Sing, who alone spoke Chinese, had it in his power to save and serve us all. Our crew consisted of seventeen men of various nations.

Awakened next morning by the hurrying to and fro of the sailors, I became uneasy, dressed in haste, and went on deck. A sailor had fallen overboard, and the ship was lying-to. His head was just visible above the waves, and we had already left him far behind. He followed us, swimming gallantly, and, in the course of about twenty minutes, came alongside, and was hoisted upon deck. His comrades greeted him with acclamations; but he replied roughly enough, as if he were ashamed of his misfortune.

Trifling as this incident was, it left an unpleasant impression on my mind; for it seemed as if our voyage had begun badly. The song of the sailors augmented my melancholy. It was a fantastic and monotonous melody, very unlike the cheerful airs sung by our French mariners. Going back sorrowfully to my cabin, I amused myself by feeding two charming little birds that I had brought with me from Hong-Kong. I kissed them tenderly; for they were all that I had to love.

The breeze was mild; we had land in sight all day, and made but little way. Towards evening the barometer fell with alarming rapidity, a strong wind sprang up, and the sea grew boisterous. Anticipating the coming storm, the captain made rapid preparations, and furled all sail. It was well he did so; for we were soon to be at the mercy of the typhoon. The typhoon is a dangerous wind, much feared in the Indian and Chinese seas. On the sea, as on the land, it carries with it death and destruction. It is neither a north wind nor a south wind, and blows as much from the east as from the west. It is, indeed, a combat between all four, and the great ocean is the scene of their warfare. Woe, then, to the ship which has to contend against this fearful strife!

Tossed and tormented, driven on from behind, and driven back from before, neither sailors nor steersmen avail to guide her.

For long hours the "Caldera" remained the plaything of this fearful wind. We were every moment threatened with destruction. Before the tempest had lasted two hours the mizen-mast and main-mast were both broken half-way, and the top-gallant masts laid along the decks, with all their cordage rent. Two of our boats had been carried away by the waves. Below, everything was broken, and we had two feet of water in the cabins. Added to all this, the waves broke against us with a noise like thunder, and our timbers creaked as if the ship would go to pieces.

Every now and then, the captain came down to console me. His hair and clothes were wet through; but, in the midst of all this danger, he never lost his cheerfulness for an instant. "You're afraid," said he, in his rough but kindly tones. I denied it; but my pale face betrayed my fears, for he shook his head compassionately as he left me.

I must confess that I endured an agony of terror. Every-thing was rolling about, and my poor little birds, hanging from the ceiling in their wicker cage, shrank down together, trembling and stupefied. For my part, I had taken refuge in my berth; for the motion was such, that I could no longer keep my footing. All at once a frightful crash resounded overhead, and I was flung out upon the floor. I covered my face with my hands – I believed that the ship was going to pieces, and that our last moments had arrived. This crash proved to be the fall of the mizen and top-gallant masts. I marvel now that the "Caldera" should have lived through the storm. She did live, however, and after fourteen hours of distress, the tempest gradually abated. Towards mid-day, the wind died quite away, and, if the sea continued to be somewhat agitated, that agitation, after what we had lately gone through, seemed like a delightful calm.

About four o'clock in the afternoon, I left my cabin and went into the saloon. It was flooded with water, and strewn with a chaotic mass of broken furniture and crockery.

I then proceeded upon deck. There, indeed, the tempest had done its work. It was with difficulty that I could make my way from one end to the other. Cables, chains, and broken masts lay about in all directions. The sea was muddy, and the sky was low, and a thick haze hung over the distance. The sailors looked weary, and one of them had been severely wounded by a falling mast. Added to our other misfortunes, fifty-two fowls and six pigs had been killed during the night. We were still within sight of land, and the captain, whose object was to get back to Hong-Kong as soon as possible, had with difficulty hoisted a sail to the foremast. To return was imperative, since it would take at least six weeks to repair the damage that we had sustained. A dead calm now reigned around us, and we remembered for the first time that we were all very hungry. Our dinner was the dreariest meal imaginable. We were all profoundly silent. The captain's face betrayed his anxiety, and I afterwards learnt that he was thinking at that very time of a misfortune which happened to him only two years before. Falling into the hands of Indian pirates, Captain Rooney had seen all his sailors killed before his face, and, being himself bound to the mast of his ship, was cruelly tortured. For three months they kept him prisoner, at the end of which time he effected his escape.

So dismal a countenance as that of the super-cargo I never beheld. He had been in mortal fear of death all through the night, and acknowledged that he had trembled almost as much for his cargo as for his life.

As for Than-Sing, his was the face of a man who openly rejoiced in his safety, and his calm smile contrasted strangely with the general uneasiness.

For my part, I could not so readily forget the sufferings of the last eighteen hours. "What more can I know of the horrors of the sea," I asked myself, "if it be not to make it my grave?"

The captain ordered us early to rest. I was so weary that I could have slept upon the floor as contentedly as upon a

feather-bed, and my berth appeared to me the most delightful place in the world. I hoped to sleep for at least ten or
twelve good hours, and had no sooner laid down than I fell
into a profound slumber.

It might have been midnight, or perhaps a little later,
when I awoke, believing myself to be the victim of a horrible nightmare. I seemed to hear a chorus of frightful cries,
and, sitting up bewildered in my bed, found my cabin filled
with a strange red light. Believing that the ship was on fire,
I sprang out of bed and rushed to the door. The captain
and the supercargo were standing each on the threshold of
his cabin. We looked speechlessly at one another, for the
savage yells grew every instant louder, and a shower of mis-
siles was falling all around. Pieces of stone and iron came
crashing down through the skylights, and rolled heavily
about the decks, and strange flashes of fire were reflected
from without.

I clung to the captain – I could not speak – I had no
voice, and the words died away upon my lips. "Captain!" I
faltered; "captain! fire! – the ship is on fire – do you hear?
– what noise is that?" But he stood like one petrified. "I do
not know," said he; and, rushing into his cabin, came back
with a revolver in his hand. That revolver was the only
weapon of defence on board. At this moment the
mate came running down. I could not hear what he said,

but, dreading some terrible misfortune, I went back into my cabin, and climbed up to the window that overlooked the sea. By the lurid light without, I beheld a crowd of Chinese junks. Beside myself with terror, I flew back to the captain, crying, "Oh, they are pirates! they are pirates!" And they were indeed pirates – those terrible pirates which scour the Chinese seas, and are so famous for their cruelties. We were utterly in their power. Three junks, each manned by thirty or forty ruffians, surrounded the "Caldera." These creatures seemed like demons, born of the tempest, and bent upon completing our destruction. Having boarded the "Caldera" by means of grappling-hooks, they were now dancing an infernal dance upon deck, and uttering cries which sounded like nothing human. The smashing of the glass awoke our whole crew, and the light which we had taken for a fire at sea was occasioned by the bursting of fiery balls which they cast on deck to frighten us. Calculating upon this method of alarming their victims, they attack vessels chiefly in the night, and seldom meet with any resistance. The captain, the super-cargo, and the mate, made an effort to go upon deck. I followed them instinctively. Driven back by flaming balls, we were forced to beat a retreat, and narrowly escaped being burnt. It seemed strange that they should risk setting fire to the ship, when plunder was their evident intention.

The captain, having but his revolver for our defence, recommended that we should keep out of sight as long as possible. Useless precaution! Accustomed as they were to predatory warfare, they were sure to find us as easily in one place as another. Fear, however, left us no time for reflection. We fled precipitately between decks, and hid ourselves as best we might. Five of the sailors were there before us, and none of us knew what had become of the rest of the crew – perhaps they were already taken prisoners. As to Than-Sing, he had not been seen since the evening before.

These savage cries, and this still more savage dance, went on overhead without cessation. Through a crack in the partition which concealed us, we witnessed all their proceedings. Seen by the red firelight, they looked unspeakably hideous. They were dressed like all other Chinese, except that they wore scarlet turbans on their heads, and round their waists broad leather belts garnished with knives and pistols. In addition to this, each man carried in his hand a naked sword. At this sight my heart sank within me, and I believed my last hour was at hand. Creeping on my hands and knees, I crouched down behind the captain, and we hid ourselves amid the merchandise, about twenty feet from the entrance. Further than this we could not go, on account of the goods which were there piled to the level of the upper deck. Scarcely able to breathe, we heard them come down into the cabins, and upset everything on which they could lay their hands. Soon a well-known voice reached our ears. It was the voice of Than-Sing, whom they had just discovered. A loud dispute then took place between him and the pirates. They doubtless demanded where the rest of the crew had hidden themselves; for he called to us in English several times, saying, "Captain, captain! where are you? Are you below? Answer! Come here! Come quickly!" But nobody stirred.

The captain grasped his pistol, and vowed to shoot the first pirate who came near us; but I entreated him to do no such thing, since the death of one man could in nowise serve us, and might, on the contrary, incline our enemies to a wholesale massacre. He seemed to see the justice of my fears, and hid his weapon in his bosom.

It was not long before we were discovered. I shudder still when I recall the sound of those approaching foot-steps. They raised the trap on deck, and let down a lighted lantern. We crowded together in a vain effort at conceal-ment; but the light came lower and lower, and we were seen at last. In another instant five or six pirates, armed to the teeth, leaped into the hold, and advanced towards us. The captain then rose up and went to meet them. Smiling, he offered them his revolver. They drew back, as if to defend themselves; then, seeing that he held the butt-end turned towards them, and that we made no effort at resistance, came eagerly forward, and glared at us with savage delight. Two of them then went up on deck, and made signs that we should follow them. More dead than alive, I remained crouched behind some bales. I saw my companions going, one by one. I would have followed them, but had no strength to stir. When the last had disappeared, and I found myself left alone with these monsters, I rose up by a despairing effort and fell at their feet. Seeing that I was a woman, they burst into exclamations of surprise and joy. Dreading every instant lest they should seize me, I rushed to the door, and in another moment found myself on deck.

Surrounded by a crowd of pirates armed with sabres and pistols, I saw every eye fixed eagerly upon the few jewels that I wore. To pull off my rings and ear-rings, and throw them at their feet, was the work of a moment, for I dreaded lest I should become the victim of their impatience. Those who were nearest clutched them greedily. An angry scuffle ensued, and but for the interference of their captain, a sanguinary quarrel would probably have followed. They then pushed me towards the stairs leading to the upper deck, and there I found my companions loaded with chains. The sea was still agitated, and huge black clouds, last remnants of the tempest, scudded hither and thither across the sky. The poor "Caldera," riding help-lessly at anchor, swayed to and fro like a mere log upon the waters. A thick fog froze us with cold, and a dead silence, which was only interrupted by the groans of the sailor who had been hurt the night before, reigned all around us. Torn by a thousand fears and regrets, I longed to weep, but could not shed a tear.

Meanwhile the pirates, who numbered, perhaps, a hundred men, were searching for plunder. Two or three of them came up, and made signs to me to observe the chains with which my companions were fettered. Thinking that they wished to treat me in the same manner, I submissively held out my hands; but they shook their heads. One of them then passed the cold blade of his sabre along my throat, whilst the others made signs expressive of their inclination to behead me. I stirred neither hand nor foot, though my face, I dare say, indicated the depth of my despair. Once more I extended my hands to be tied. They seized hold of them angrily, and passed their fingers round and round my wrists, though for what purpose I could not imagine. What could they want? Was it their intention to cut off my hands? In this moment I recognized all the horrors of my position. I closed my eyes, and leaned my head against the bulwark. The sight of these monsters was alone sufficient to make death welcome, and I awaited it with entire resignation. I was still in this state of semi-stupefaction when Than-Sing came up, and touched me on the shoulder. "Be not afraid," said he; "they do not mean to harm you. Their only object is to frighten you, lest you should attempt to set your companions at liberty."

He was now sent for by the pirate-chief, who was a small wiry-looking man, with a countenance more intelligent and less ferocious than the others. Than-Sing, although not fettered, was a prisoner like ourselves, and, being the only Chinese on board, acted as our interpreter.

Captain Rooney was next sent for. Calm and disdainful, he seemed to despise the success of his captors and his own personal danger. "Is he English?" asked the chief. Than-Sing, luckily remembering the feud then existing between China and Great Britain, replied that the captain was a Spaniard, and the crew composed of various Europeans. This proved, indeed, to be a fortunate inspiration; for the pirate instantly replied that, had we been English, our throats should all have been cut upon the spot. He then enquired respecting the number of persons on board, and the amount of money which we carried, and ended by asking if I were the wife of Mr. Rooney. Having satisfied him on the two former points, Than-Sing replied that I was a Frenchwoman, journeying to California, a stranger in China, and quite without friends or relatives in this part of the world. The excellent Chinese was careful to impress this fact of my loneliness upon them, hoping thereby to moderate any expectations which they might have formed respecting the amount of my ransom.

Captain Rooney's hands were then released, and he had to submit to the humiliation of accompanying the chief through every part of the ship. He was even obliged to furnish an exact inventory of his cargo. For our lives we were already indebted to the generous misrepresentations of Than-Sing; but it was yet possible that the pirates might change their minds, and although they had promised to save our lives, we scarcely dared to depend upon it. Besides all this, more pirates might arrive to dispute the prize, and we be sacrificed in the strife. Such were my reflections during the absence of the captain. A scene of plunder was at this moment being enacted before my eyes. The cabins were first dismantled; and I beheld my own luggage transported on board the junks. Everything was taken – even my dear little birds in their wicker cage. "They survived the tempest," said I, "only to die of cold and neglect!" And, with this, the tears which had so long refused to flow, coursed hotly down my cheeks.

I was aroused from this melancholy train of thought by the return of the captain. Our sailors were now unchained to work the ship, and the pirate-chief gave orders that we should weigh anchor, and put into a neigh-bouring bay. At the same time our men were all given to understand that, at the least token of revolt, we should all be slaughtered without pity. As for Than-Sing, the super-cargo, and myself, we were left on the upper deck in company with the wounded sailor, since none of us could be of use in the management of the vessel.

At this moment one of the robbers came up with a parcel of jewels and money, which he had just found. In one hand he held a silver fork, the properties and uses of which seemed mightily to perplex him. He paused, looked at me, and raised the fork to his head, as if to ask me whether it were a woman's comb. Under any other circum-stances his ignorance might have amused me; now, however, I had no strength to reply to him even by a sign. Than-Sing then came to my assistance, and the pirate, having received the information he desired, went away. I hoped that we had got rid of him, but returning almost immediately, he held a handful of silver before my eyes, pointed towards a junk which we had in tow, and endeavoured, by his looks and gestures, to arouse me from my apathy. It was not dif-ficult to interpret these signs, and I saw with a shudder that he wanted me to fly with him. Than-Sing, who had been silently observing this scene, now took pity on my distress, and addressed the man in Chinese. He doubtless threatened to betray his treachery to the chief; for the pirate hung his head, and went silently away.

The weather was now misty, and much colder; and, half-clothed as we were, we suffered intensely. It is but fair, however, to say that our captors were not wholly insensible to our miseries, and that they had at least the charity to cover us with a few rugs and pieces of sail-cloth.

Shortly after this, we heard a sound of falling chains, and the anchor was cast once more. Alas! was that anchor ever to be weighed again, or was it destined to rust away throughout all the ages of time, in the spot where it was now imbedded? Heaven only knew!

CHAPTER VI

D AY broke, and the last shades of night faded
and fled. The pirates assembled us on deck,
counted us over to see that none were missing,
lifted the hatches at the foot of the mainmast, and
lowered us, one by one, into the hold. Some of
them followed us down, and kept a savage watch
upon our every movement. This last proceeding
struck us with a mortal terror. Believing that our
fate was just about to be decided, we sat down

mournfully among the bales of goods, and waited like condemned criminals. Our jailers seemed now to be more cruelly disposed than ever. Every moment, and without any kind of provocation, they struck our poor sailors with the handles and flats of their sabres, and amused themselves by flourishing these weapons round my head and that of Captain Rooney. Presently they took to examining our wrists, and laughed to see the wounds which our chains had left upon them. Hearing a noise on deck, they, by and bye, left us; having first taken the precaution of battening down the hatches above our heads. Plunged into utter darkness, and almost suffocated for want of air, we endured this captivity for more than an hour. The hatches were then lifted, a flood of blinding sunlight poured in upon us, and the friendly voice of Than-Sing greeted us from above.

Up to the present time, as I have already shown, the Chinese merchant had had it in his power to render us important services. Of these he never wearied. He was our good genius. His presence alone inspired us with courage and endurance; and whenever he opened his mouth to interpose between our feebleness and the ferocity of his countrymen, our dangers seemed to diminish. His coolness never failed him for an instant. When he was not actually with us, pursuing his work of encouragement and comfort, he was negotiating in our favour. With that expression of calm serenity, his plain features became at times almost patriarchal; and I was amazed to find any Chinese gifted with qualities of such Christian charity.

During the hour which had just gone by, the question of life and death had probably been debated. Providence, however, had watched over us, and we were once more spared. It was now decided by the pirate-chief that our crew should be set to work to unlade the vessel.

The valuable freight of opium which we had on board was the property of Than-Sing, who was accordingly sent below with Captain Rooney to assist the pirates in clearing out these stores. The sailors then passed the packages from hand to hand; the pirates formed a chain from junk to junk; and the bales of sugar, rice, coffee, and other goods were speedily transferred.

Forgotten in the midst of this excitement, I sat alone and watched the work of spoilation.

After about an hour's labour, our sailors were allowed to rest for a few moments, and received a scanty ration of biscuits and water. Several of the poor fellows offered me a share of their food; but, although I eagerly drank what water they could spare me, I found it impossible to eat a morsel. For long hours my throat and chest had been on fire, and I suffered cruelly from thirst.

Soon after this, Than-Sing and the captain came in search of me. Thankful was I, indeed, to see them; for the pirates had of late been thronging around me with gesticulations which filled me with uneasiness. My friends then led me to a cabin, at the other end of the vessel, where I hoped to be left without molestation. Crossing the deck, I saw that we had anchored close in shore, and were surrounded by an immense amphitheatre of wooded hills. At any other time I should have been charmed with this exquisite scene; but the sight of the "Caldera," now a mere wreck, usurped all my attention. Her broken masts were lying along deck – fragments of doors and windows lay scattered all about – the compass had been carried away, and the helm was broken. Add to this the ferocious cries of our barbarian captors, and the picture is complete. I was glad to hurry away from this sight; but our pretty cabins were no longer recognizable. Lying upon a large green velvet sofa, which was the only article of furniture left entire, I yielded to an access of the profoundest of melancholy. Every moment the pirates kept passing to and fro, or coming in to cast lots for such of the booty as was yet unshared amongst them. Remembering how they had refused to tie my hands, and the little likelihood I had for supposing them to be actuated by any feeling of compassion or respect, I recalled some frightful stories read in times gone by, and dreaded lest I should become the victim of their brutality. Sooner than this, I resolved to throw myself into the sea. That I should now be living to write these lines – that I should now be relating the long story of my sufferings – seems, if I may dare to say so, like a special manifestation of that divine goodness which measures the trial by the strength of the sufferer.

Our provisions, with the exception of some rice and a few biscuits, had all been carried on board the three junks. Our sailors had been allowed no rest. Groaning under fatigues, which were enforced with the sword, they laboured on till night-fall, and even then, but for the intercessions of Than-Sing, would have been allowed no sleep.

My companions slept in the cabin adjoining mine, and we were allowed to close our doors for the night. Having eaten nothing all day, and being kept awake, moreover, by the vociferations of the pirates, whose numbers had lately been increased by the arrival of fresh junks, I passed a miserable night. Many a time, during these long hours of wakefulness, I opened my little window and leaned out into the air; but each time that I did so, my terrors were increased by the sight of these demons quarrelling over their booty. Day dawned, and a sudden rumour spread all at once throughout the ship. Starting from their sleep, our sailors rushed on deck, and two or three came down crying, "The pirates are leaving us! The pirates are leaving us!" A wild and sudden hope possessed us. We believed that help was at hand, and that the moment of our release had arrived. Could it be the approach of a steamer which caused the flight of our captors? A single glance, however, was sufficient. Alas! that which we had supposed to be a deliverance, proved to be but an added danger. Our pirates were indeed leaving us, but a new flotilla was bearing down upon us with all sail set! For more than a quarter of an hour we were left alone in the wreck, and Than-Sing explained to us that the small junks were making off with their booty, for fear it should be wrested from them by the new comers. These second enemies were, then, fiercer and more numerous than the first! What would they do with us? What would now become of us? What had we to expect? We counted the minutes as they passed, and the junks drew rapidly nearer. I felt my very heart sink within me, and all the horrors to which I might be subjected rushed across my mind. "Oh, captain," said I, "I shall die with fear! Can you not help to disguise me? Let me be dressed as you are! What shall I do? I am a woman, and these monsters are coming! Have pity on me! Have pity on me!" "Yes, you are right," said Captain Rooney, kindly and compassionately. Having on two pairs of trousers, he then gave me one. We next found a shirt and a Chinese jacket, and one of the sailors gave me his cap, beneath which I gathered up my hair. I had but one hair-pin left, and on my naked feet a pair of slippers. Hastening into my cabin, I dressed rapidly, and had scarcely completed this transformation when loud shouts proclaimed the approach of our new enemies. The small junks, which had fled before the others like startled water-fowl, were already far away. We hid ourselves in one of the after-cabins, and the captain grouped his men in such a manner as might best conceal me. He and Than-Sing stood before me, and in another moment the pirates were on board. About forty junks now surrounded the "Caldera," each junk carrying from twenty to forty men, and the large ones being mostly mounted with ten or twelve cannons.

The pirates of the Chinese seas make their junks their homes, and carry their wives and children with them on every expedition. The women assist in working the ships, and are chiefly employed in lading and unlading the merchandise. As for the children, they carry them upon their backs in a kind of bag, till they are able to run alone. Each junk is commanded by a chief, and such is the terror of the pirate-name, that, in a country which numbers three hundred and sixty millions of inhabitants, they ravage the seas with im-punity. It sometimes happens that they have feuds among themselves, and many a piratical sea-fight takes place, in which the victory rests with the strongest.

Hidden as we were in a lower cabin, we heard these barbarians rush upon our decks, with the force of a torrent that had burst its flood-gates. The first junks having carried away but a small portion of our cargo, these new pirates found an ample prize remaining. They therefore employed themselves in pillaging the ship, without taking the trouble to seek for us. Presently, such of the junks as were sufficiently laden, dropped away, and set sail for those villages along the coast, where they were in the habit of taking refuge. In the meantime, despite the indifference with which they treated us, fresh fears assailed us. We dreaded lest they should exhaust our store of provisions, and found ere long that these apprehensions were but too well grounded. Soon, a sack of rice, and a small bag of biscuits alone remained, and even these they would have taken from us, but for our urgent supplications. We were now utterly destitute. For two days and more, we could scarcely be said to have eaten anything, and, faint with exhaustion, we abandoned ourselves to despair. As if animated with the very spirit of destruction, the pirates demolished every-thing which came in their way. The panellings in the saloon, the looking-glasses, the windows, the doors, and such of the furniture as was not already destroyed, they smashed into a thousand pieces. They carried away the very hinges and fastenings from off the doors, and even the green velvet divan, which had hitherto been left on account of its size. The deck was strewn all over with tea, coffee, sugar, biscuit, fragments of broken glass, and merchandise. We were constantly obliged to turn out our pockets, in proof that we kept nothing back; and these monsters pressed around us, every now and then, in such numbers that we could scarcely move or breathe. My dress, which I had hidden as best I could, was found and carried off like everything else; and Than-Sing, who had chanced to take off his slippers for a moment, saw them snatched up and appropriated in the twinkling of an eye. The poor man was more annoyed by this loss, than by all his previous misfortunes; for the slippers were made after the fashion of his country. Hereafter, one of our sailors, who was indifferently skilful in such matters, contrived to make him a new pair, out of some fragments of leather which he found about the deck.

Cast upon the mercy of these savages, our situation was inexpressibly horrible. They were not deceived by my costume; for they surrounded me with eager curiosity, and asked Than-Sing if I were the wife of the captain. These questions filled me with terror, and I entreated Mr. Rooney to let me pass for his wife. They gathered round us in brutal mockery, asking if we wished to go to Hong-Kong; and then, finding that we were silent, laughed in our faces. Some of them, who seemed more savage and cruel than the rest, seized our sailors by the hair, and flourished their sabres threateningly before their eyes; whilst I, sinking, and sick at heart, shrank down in a corner, and hoped to be forgotten. Slender indeed was the tenure upon which we now hold our lives! Who knows what might have happened had one single drop of blood been actually shed?

That same day, one of these men came, when none of the rest were by, and talked for some time to Than-Sing. I saw the merchant's face light up as the conversation progressed, and the breathless eagerness with which he replied. The pirate was offering, as I afterwards learnt, to effect our escape; and Captain Rooney, by help of Than-Sing, agreed on the amount of our ransom. We were to be landed at Hong-Kong, and, meanwhile, were desired to hold ourselves in readiness for the first chance of escape. Two others came shortly after upon the same errand; but, whether the reward which we offered was insufficient to recompense them for the danger, or whether they dreaded the discovery of their treason, I know not – at all events, not one of the three kept his word, and we saw them no more.

Towards the evening of this day our sailors complained bitterly of hunger. We feared being left to all the agonies of starvation; but, in the midst of our distress, help came whence we had least reason to expect it. Amongst these robbers there was one who seemed actuated by sentiments of compassion. He came to us every now and then, appeared to sympathize with our distress, and, by and bye, pointed out his wife and children on board a neighbouring junk. Pleased to observe the interest with which we looked upon his family, this pirate, at the very moment when we were deploring our hunger, came back with a dish of rice and a huge bowl filled with some kind of Chinese *ragoût,* dressed after the Chinese fashion, with a thick saffron-coloured sauce. Our poor fellows, little used to dainties, devoured it eagerly. But I could only just touch it with my lips, for the odour of it disgusted me. I contrived, however, to alleviate my hunger with a few spoonfuls of the rice. Towards night, the junks let go the grappling-irons, and put out to sea. It seemed scarcely probable that they would return again in equal numbers, since our plundered state must soon become known throughout the pirate-villages which line that coast.

Their departure left us at least the prospect of a quiet night; but, on the other hand, our ship was dismantled, and we had no available means of action. Had our enemies indeed abandoned us to die slowly of hunger, exposed to all the burning heat of a tropical sun, and swayed helplessly to and fro upon the great ocean, thousands of leagues from our homes and families? Than-Sing had ascertained that we were about twenty miles from Macao. Far away, he said, between two mountains which were just visible on the horizon, lay the city. This knowledge only served to make us still more miserable. Life was there, safety was there, and yet we could do nothing to help ourselves! If even we had succeeded in weighing the anchor, what chance had we, in our dismasted state, of drifting into any place of shelter? Glad to forget our anxieties, if but for a few hours, we all lay down to sleep.

What a picture it was! We had constructed a kind of rude oil-lamp, which cast a flickering glare around the cabin. This room, once so cheerful and pretty, now more nearly resembled some hideous dungeon. Seeing these rough sailors stretched about the floor, these upturned faces weary with suffering, these dismantled walls, and this air of general desolation, I began almost to tremble for my reason. Being so wretched, what more had I to fear? What were death to one whose sufferings had already touched the bounds of human endurance? One by one, my companions sank away to sleep, and I alone remained, wakeful and sorrowful, to meditate the chances of our destiny. I questioned my past life; I searched all the corners of my memory; I asked myself what I had done to merit this great trial? Gladly would I have discovered any fault deserving such retribution, for I could not endure to doubt the justice of Heaven.

It might now have been about ten o'clock at night. I had tried in vain to sleep, and could not keep my eyes closed for five minutes together. Torn by a thousand different emotions, I lay and listened to the silence, till, carried away by an irresistible excitement, I rose, made my way on deck, and, flinging myself wearily down, gazed up at the sky and the stars. The moon shone like a silver mirror, and, seeing the stillness and solitude of the night, I could not help fancying that something might yet be done towards our deliverance. Going back into the cabin, I roused Captain Rooney, and entreated him to come with me on deck. Somewhat surprised at this request, he rose and followed me. No sooner had we gone up, than we heard a sound of voices close under our lee, and found that a small junk was still lying alongside of us. The captain eagerly bent forward, as if to count the number of our enemies. They could not have been more than eight or ten. Having attentively observed them, he became profoundly silent. Amazed at his apathy, I dragged him towards the jolly-boat, which was yet hanging amidships, and said, "Well, captain, why do you not rouse your men?" He looked at me with a kind of weary wonder, as if scarcely able to comprehend my meaning. "Will you then do nothing?" said I. "Are you content patiently to await all the horrors of the future? Woman as I am, I would prefer a thousand times to dare something for my safety, than linger here to die by violence or starvation! We are but twenty miles from Macao. This boat will hold us all. Once at sea, it is scarcely likely that the pirates, busy as they are, will observe our flight. Should they even see us, they might no longer care to follow us. Captain, in the name of all that is dear to you, let us at least make the attempt!"

Captain Rooney paused, remained for a few moments lost in thought, and then went quickly back into the cabin. "Rouse up!" said he, "rouse up, all of you! How can you sleep while we are yet in so much danger?" Laying aside his old habits of command, he then consulted them respecting our common danger, and suggested a plan of escape. At the first word of this proposition, the sailors turned disobediently away. "You do not deserve the name of men," said the captain, angrily. "I blush to think that a woman should be braver than you! She has the courage to prefer death to delay; and, while flight yet offers us some chance of safety, you hesitate, you tremble, you behave like cowards! I see fear in every eye! No, I repeat it – no, you have not even the courage of a woman!"

Captain Rooney's plan was this: he proposed that his crew should steal softly upon deck, take the junk by surprise, and slay the eight Chinese by whom it was manned. We might then, without loss of time, set sail for Macao, where we should, in all probability, arrive before daybreak.

I remained silent whilst this consultation was going forward. My wisest course was to remain passive, in order that these men should not have it in their power to say that I proposed such bloodshed. That they did so accuse me was sufficiently plain, and yet I protest that in this suggestion I had no share whatever. The captain had not confided his projects to me; he had simply relied on my courage and co-operation, and had held me up to the men as an example for the mere sake of putting them to shame.

"Captain," said the supercargo, glancing angrily towards me, "that woman is mad; and, if it be by her advice that you are acting, we but consult the dictates of reason in refusing to obey you. This attempt could end only in destruction. Granting that we succeeded in capturing the junk, we should assuredly be overtaken, in the night, by others of the pirates, and they, guessing the means by which we had obtained possession of their cursed junk, would slay us all, without mercy."

There was justice in what he said; and the captain then fell back upon the plan which I had first proposed. It was agreed that the boat should be emptied of the coals with which it was now half-filled, and lowered into the water. While the men were busy at this work, I wandered to and fro about the deck, and, searching amidst the *débris*, found some fragments of my dear home-letters. They were all torn and soiled, and I gathered them together with a sigh. At this moment, as if for the very purpose of favouring our flight, the last junk put off, and hove away to sea, leaving us alone for the first time since our captivity. Being now enabled to work with less precaution, the men redoubled their efforts, and the boat was soon unloaded. Eagerly and anxiously we crowded round, and examined it. Alas, how great was our disappointment! Several planks had started in the bottom of the boat, and she was no longer sea-worthy. Intense as was their discouragement, our sailors persisted in the attempt. A dull splash followed. We hung over the side of the vessel, and breathlessly prayed to Heaven for help and protection.

Ten minutes thus passed by. "It cannot be done," said the captain, falteringly; "she is already half-full of water." We looked into each others faces, and silently dispersed. Great sorrows are dumb. Till tomorrow nothing could now be done, and who could tell what that morrow might bring forth?

CHAPTER VII

*Efforts at Escape – Attempted Flight – Return to the
"Caldera" – Capture – Cruelties of the Pirates –
Portrait of a Pirate Chief – Chinese Prayer – Death of
a Pirate – Seizure of a Merchant Junk – Fresh Plunder
– Fortune of the Vanquished.*

ON the following day our sailors set to work
gallantly. To repair the jolly-boat would
take, at the least, eight or ten hours of hard labour,
and our only hope lay in the continued absence of
our enemies. The greater part of the day went by
thus, and for hours and hours no sail was visible
on the horizon. Once more we had the "Caldera"
to ourselves; but she was now a mere shell,

dismantled, melancholy, and motionless – a floating mass of utter ruin! We fixed ten o'clock at night for the moment of our escape, and throughout all the day toiled on without any kind of food or rest. But for the nervous energy which kept me up, I know not how I should have borne this long starvation; as it was, my strength was failing rapidly.

To fit a mast to the boat, and construct some kind of rude sail out of the rags that lay strewn about our decks, occupied the men up to a late hour of the evening. As all our rigging had been either carried away, or cut to pieces, they even contrived to make some bamboo canes serve in the place of ropes. This done, we prepared to leave the ship, and were just about to lower the boat, when two junks came into sight, and bore down straight upon us. Stowing away all that could be hidden of our preparations, we hastened to take refuge in our cabins, and there awaited whatever might happen.

It was not long before they hove alongside, and they had no sooner leapt on board, than they came down in search of us. Two of the pirates carried lanterns, by the light of which they examined us one by one, as if to make sure that none were missing. Arrived where I lay hidden behind some of my companions, they laughed, and called to each other with every mark of satisfaction. One made signs to me to rise, but I could only look up imploringly, and had no strength to stir. Another, irritated, perhaps, by my languor, threatened me with his sabre, which only added to my terror, and left me more helpless than ever. But for an agonized cry, which just then drew their attention from me towards one of their number, who had missed his footing and fallen into the hold, I hardly know now how this scene might have ended. Having pitched from the deck to the very bottom of the vessel, the Chinese was brought up by one of our sailors. More dead than alive, he lay and groaned piteously, and the pirates, being occupied with his sufferings, and pleased, to all appearance, with the ready help which our men had afforded him, tormented and threatened me no more.

Our alarms, however, were not yet ended. These barbarians seemed to delight in our terror; and, not content with all that they had already done, now took it into their heads to carry lighted torches into the hold, and all about the cabins, thereby scattering a shower of sparks in every direction, and more than once setting fire to the chips and rubbish that lay heaped around. Had not our sailors followed, and stamped out the sparks as they fell, the wreck must soon have been in flames. Weary at length of this ferocious pastime, the pirates returned to their junks, put out to sea, and left us once more in peace.

Thankful to be released from their presence, our brave fellows flew to work again, and rigged the jolly-boat afresh. She was still somewhat leaky; but we had made up our minds to sink or starve at sea, sooner than die at last by the hands of the pirates. At this solemn moment, we were unanimous in our courage and our hope. Not one of us but preferred drowning in the bosom of the deep sea, to the chances of starvation or massacre. Not one of us but left his fate to Heaven, and was content to venture, be the end what it might! In the meantime, the weather, which had hitherto been all that we could desire, became less favourable to our purpose. The sky, last night so serene, grew low and cloudy, and the wind, which had up to this time been blowing to the shore, shifted quite round, and seemed to forbid our progress. Seeing these signs of bad weather, the captain shook his head doubtfully; but our minds were made up. We had resolved to go, and would not be delayed.

It had now become a matter of some difficulty to get down into the boat; for, being gutted of her cargo, the "Caldera" necessarily drew but little water, and floated so high above the sea-level, as to leave an immense distance between the ship's deck and the jolly-boat. The wounded sailor and I were then lowered by means of cords, and the others, being more agile, contrived to clamber down in safety. The captain then placed himself at the helm; the supercargo, the Chinese merchant, the sick man, and myself were seated near him; the sailors grasped the rude oars which they had themselves constructed; and, twenty-two in number, we put out to sea. From the first moment of our starting, two sailors were constantly baling out the water that made its way through the bottom of the boat; and, as Captain Rooney had already anticipated, our sail soon proved to be worse than useless, and had to be taken down.

Struggling against a contrary breeze, and driven back by every wave that met us, we made but little progress. Looking back towards the "Caldera," I seemed to see its sombre outline loom larger through the mist the farther we left it behind. High above the waves, like a huge hearse, floated that dreary hulk. Alas! we strove in vain to fly from it. To row in such a sea would have been difficult under the most ordinary circumstances; and, weak and wearied as they were, our men could make no head against the waves. Their oars, rough-hewn during the day, were too heavy to be manageable. Washed over every moment by the waves, the boat filled rapidly with water, and four men could scarcely bale it out fast enough for our safety. Besides all this, an icy wind blew from the north, and the hands of the rowers grew numbed and nerveless. We went three miles in this manner. Then, after four hours of super-human effort, our sailors quite broke down, and confessed that they could do no more. It was the will of Heaven. The "Caldera" seemed destined to become our tomb.

"Let us return," said the captain, hoarsely, and he looked, as he said this, like one who believes himself in the hands of fate, and hopes no more from either God or man.

"Yes, let us go back," I replied. "Death can be but welcome after sufferings like these."

The current, which had been hitherto our greatest enemy, bore us back, almost without an effort on our part, to the very spot from which we had started. The rope by which we had been let down, was swinging to and fro as we had left it. The others caught hold of it and climbed easily enough, but it was with the utmost difficulty that the invalid and I were hoisted on board.

I no sooner found myself standing, once again, upon this fatal deck, than everything swam before my eyes, and I fell heavily to the ground. Pain and hunger were fast doing their work upon me, and the very principle of life was ebbing from my heart. It was long before I recovered my consciousness, and, when I opened my eyes, I found that I was laid upon a bench and surrounded by kindly faces. Every man had deprived himself of some article of clothing to warm and cover me. Having but water to give, they gave it. Such cares as were in their power to bestow they lavished on me; and so called me back to life at the very moment when it would have been most sweet to die. Some of them wept. Perhaps, looking at me, they thought of the wives, the mothers, the sisters, whom they had left at home.

Finding that I was now somewhat revived, my companions stretched themselves on the floor, and slept till morning. I also slept; but my dreams were of that dear France which I never hoped to see again, and, more than once, my own hot tears awoke me.

The next day was the 11th of October. I had slept for some hours, and this brief rest had for awhile effaced the remembrance of my sufferings. Starting up, however, in the early morning, I had no sooner opened my eyes than all the dread reality was brought before me. There, close beside me, stood a group of armed Chinese, and, in the midst of them, Than-Sing, eagerly conversing. He who seemed to be their leader, pointed towards me with his finger. I looked on in speechless stupefaction. Captain Rooney then came up, and Than-Sing, who still acted as our interpreter, explained the nature of the conference. "Captain," said he, "the chief is about to carry you and me, and this French lady, to Macao, where he hopes to get a heavy ransom for us." Captain Rooney bowed his head in melancholy acquiescence, and prepared to submit. I was immediately lifted by some two or three pirates and carried upon deck; but I scarcely comprehended what had been said, or whither they were taking me. Than-Sing went first; and I, being helped down a wretched ladder, followed him. I then looked up, expecting to see Captain Rooney next on his way; but found, to my horror, that the pirates had snatched the ladder away, and pushed off without him! No words can depict the shock with which I beheld this last act of treachery. Leaving Canton, I had been recommended to his care, and in all our troubles he had watched over me with the gentlest solicitude. He was my protector – my friend; and, parted from him, I believed myself lost beyond redemption. I held out my arms in token of adieu, and saw the stony wonder in his face.

"Take me with you!" he cried, passionately; "Oh, take me with you!"

Then, seeing that it was useless, he covered his face with his hands, and wept bitterly.

We were summoned, some few minutes after, to the cabin of the chief, who told Than-Sing that Captain Rooney was presently to be forwarded to Hong-Kong or Macao, there to negotiate for our ransoms and his own. "In seven or eight days," said he, "all will be arranged. In the meantime you must stay with us as hostages."

We were not suffered to remain in the chief's cabin, but had to cross the deck and go on to the after-part of the vessel. I looked eagerly round, in the hope of seeing the "Caldera" for the last time; but we were already far away, and she was no longer visible.

The pirates who had us in charge then lifted a kind of trap, about two feet square, and pushed us down into a narrow dark hole below deck, where we had no room to stand upright, and could with difficulty lie at full length. When we sat, our heads touched the flooring above. The trap being left open, we could at least breathe the fresh air, and look up to the sky; but, once shut in, our only light proceeded from a tiny port-hole of some eight inches square, which looked out beside the moving helm, and was not made to open. We had not lain more than half an hour in this dreary place, when a heavy blow echoed above our heads, followed by many others in rapid succession. Our eyes met, and each read the same dark suspicion in the other's face. Was it possible that they were nailing down the trap above our heads? Was this hole destined to be our coffin and our tomb? Had we been separated from our companions only to die slowly of hunger, thirst, and suffocation? A cold chill ran over all my body – I struggled to my knees – I strove, weak as I was, to force the lid up with my feeble hands. Oh, it was despair and anguish unspeakable!

"It is thus," I thought, "that they suffer who are buried alive!"

This idea was too much for my reason. My brain burned – I lost all self-control – I strove to dash my head against the wall, and put an end to my miseries. In the midst of my delirium, I felt two hands pressing mine, and saw Than-Sing bending over me, with the tears streaming down his cheeks. He entreated me to be calm; and presently I also wept, and strove to wait my fate with resignation. Thus two frightful hours went by; and then, as if by enchantment, the trap was suddenly raised, and the blessed sunlight flowed in once more upon us. It was, but a cruel jest, and they had only feigned to nail us in, after all!

They crowded round the opening, laughing and pointing at us; and then, when their curiosity was satisfied, would have closed it up again, but for the prayers and representations of my companion. They then consented to leave about two inches open, and having taken advantage of this opportunity to rise and change our position, we lay at full length along the floor, and breathed, at least, a less polluted air.

Towards evening they brought us a small bucketful of water, with which we washed our hands and faces; also some dried fish, some rice, and a little tea. So weak was I, that my head seemed too heavy for my body, and I now loathed the very sight of food. But Than-Sing ate eagerly, and implored me to partake of some little nourishment. Above all, he counselled me not to seem mistrustful of our foes, or of the food they gave us. Thus urged, I contrived to eat half a saucer of rice, and drink a little tea; but even this cost me a painful effort, and a degree of emotion for which I find it difficult to account. It grew dark about eight o'clock in the evening, and just as night was closing in, we heard an infernal yelling upon deck. Than-Sing hastened to reassure me. "It is the hour of prayer," said he. "Prayer!" I repeated. "Do these monsters pray?"

By and bye, I shall have something more to tell of their religious ceremonies.

When it was quite dark, the pirates summoned Than-Sing upon deck. Coming back some few minutes after, they told me that I also might go up to take the air. We were now anchored not far from land, in the neighbourhood of several other junks, the crews of which were all at prayer. It seemed strange, in the presence of this calm sea and silver starlight, to hear the dull echoing of the gongs and drums, and the rude cries of the worshippers. This moment of brief liberty was inexpressibly delightful, and it seemed as if the sight of all-giving Nature might, even then, have consoled me, but for the necessity of returning to my prison. During the long hours that followed, I could think only of my misfortunes, and deemed myself comparatively happy in being associated with one whose age and benevolence placed him upon almost a paternal footing.

I had confidence in Than-Sing, and, witnessing his unshaken stedfastness, looked upon him as my protector. He consoled me; he looked upon me as a daughter. "While I have him by my side," thought I, "he will, perhaps, interpose between me and my enemies, whatever be their designs. Then, should he be taken from me, I can at least throw myself into the sea."

One of the pirates now brought us a light, which consisted of a little wick in a saucer of oil. Feeble as it was, it yet sufficed to light up the walls of our narrow dungeon. Scarcely had I looked round, when I uttered a cry of horror. Ceiling, walls, and floor were peopled by a multitude of huge velvety spiders, enormous beetles, and monstrous wood-lice, horned and shiny. In another instant, three or four great rats rushed out of a corner, and ran between my feet. Seeing my disgust, Than-Sing offered to put out the light; but I preferred the sight of these reptiles to the torture of hearing and feeling them in the darkness of night. Fortunately, I still had a pocket-handkerchief remaining. With this I covered my head and face, and, hiding my hands under my clothes, crouched motionless in the middle of the floor throughout the remainder of the night. Towards morning the vermin disappeared.

Not long after daybreak, we were again supplied with provisions, and with a bucket of water, in which we washed our hands and faces. Than-Sing then informed me that the Chinese never eat till they have performed their morning's ablution. As before, our food consisted of rice, fish, and tea. With these they sent us two pairs of tiny chop-sticks, each about a foot in length, and as thick as an ordinary pencil. The Chinese hold them as we hold a pen, and handle them with the utmost dexterity. Notwithstanding all the patience and skill with which Than-Sing endeavoured to teach me the use of these little sticks, I found them so impracticable as to be obliged at last to give up the attempt, and eat with my fingers.

Today, again, the pirates came to watch and mock at us. One of them, more insulting than the rest, pointed first at me and then at the Chinese merchant, and represented the action of two persons embracing. This cowardly insult pained me more than all their previous cruelties. I felt myself become scarlet with shame and anger, and gave way to a passion of tears. In the midst of my distress the pirate-captain happened to pass by, and, as if moved by my affliction, ordered the trap to be closed above our heads.

This chief, unlike his men, had something not wholly disagreeable in the expression of his countenance. He alone inspired me with neither disgust nor terror. His ugliness was, so to say, individual. His face was long and thin; he had high cheek-bones, a wide mouth, a short flat nose with open nostrils, dark eyebrows, and very large black eyes. His head was closely shaved, excepting on the crown, whence grew a long thick tress, which he wore sometimes clubbed on the nape of the neck; sometimes plaited, and bound round his head like a coronet; and sometimes hanging down his back, a yard or more in length. Transformed as he was by these various styles, his face always preserved a certain pleasant character. His consideration on the present occasion inspired me now with some hope for the future.

Than-Sing, partly to amuse me, partly to set my mind at rest, repeated to me the questions and observations which the pirates had addressed to him. They had asked him the number of his wives, which, in China, is a standard of wealth; and then added that if our ransoms were not sufficiently heavy, they would make a pirate of him, and give me in marriage to one of their companions. Seeing me now look more distressed than ever, the good merchant explained that the men of his country were not permitted to intermarry with aliens, and that these threats were only feints to draw him into conversation. "Be careful, however," said he, "never to lay your hand upon me in their presence. It is contrary to our custom, and they might repeat it to my disadvantage." To all their other questions he had replied that he was only a poor man, about to seek his fortune in California, and gave them to understand that he was working out a cheap passage on board the "Caldera." He was, therefore, careful to avoid any allusion which might lead them to conjecture the extent of his means. Had they supposed him wealthy, they would not only have quadrupled his ransom, but might even have put him to the torture. He then spoke to me of his family. He had but one wife, he said, and his home was in Canton. He was the father of three daughters, of eight, eighteen, and twenty-five years of age, the eldest of whom was married. He seemed to love them tenderly, and wept when he spoke of them. He scarcely hoped ever to see them again, and had but little belief in our ultimate deliverance. I often enquired of him, at this time, respecting the manners and customs of the pirates; to which he always replied, shudderingly, that they were not to be depended upon, and were dangerously fond of decapitating their prisoners.

The following day went by without any event of interest. I only remember that the pirates questioned Than-Sing about my name and country; and, having learned these facts by heart, amused themselves by perpetually shouting "Fanny! Fanny!" which often startled me.

I became miserably cramped towards evening; and Than-Sing entreated permission for me to remain upon deck somewhat longer than usual. They consented, and I thereby had an opportunity of witnessing the ceremonies of their evening prayer.

Every junk, like every Chinese house, is furnished with an altar. On this altar they burn small wax-lights, and offer up oblations of meat and drink. They pray every night at the same hour, and begin with a hideous overture played upon gongs, cymbals, and drums covered with serpent skins.

First of all, I saw a young Chinese come forward with two swords, which he stuck upright in the very centre of the deck. Beside these he then placed some saucers, a vase filled with liquid, and a bundle of spills, made of yellow paper, and intended for burning. A lighted lantern was next suspended to one of the masts, and the chief fell upon his knees before the shrine. After chanting for some time, he took up the vase and drank; and next proceeded, with many gesticulations, to chink a lot of coins and medals together in his hands. The paper spills were then lighted and carried round and round the swords, as if to consecrate them. These ceremonies completed, the captain rose from his knees, came down to the after-part of the junk, waved the burning papers to and fro, and threw them solemnly into the sea. The gongs and drums were now played more loudly, and the chief seemed to pray more earnestly than ever; but as soon as the last paper was dropped, and the last spark extinguished, the music ceased, the prayer came to an end, and the service was over. Altogether it had taken quite twenty minutes, and I had gained all that time in the open air.

That night I strove in vain to sleep. The insects which infested our dungeon tormented me incessantly, and my feet were blistered all over from their bites. The rats, also, which at first had fled before the sound of our voices, were now grown but too friendly, and ran over us in broad daylight, as we were lying on the floor.

It was now the thirteenth day of the month. The junk still coasted along close in shore, and our position was as yet in nowise altered. In the evening we heard a great commotion upon deck, and found that one of the pirates had fallen overboard. Not having perceived this accident until

too late, the man was quite dead by the time they succeeded in picking him up. They laid the corpse so close
beside the opening to our cell, that the water came streaming from it full upon our heads. After a quarter of an hour
of confusion, they gave up all hope of bringing him back
to life, and, with sullen imprecations, flung the body back
into the sea.

On the morning of the 15th, we came up with several
other pirate-junks, and joined them in giving chase to a
merchant-junk, plying between Hong-Kong and Canton
with goods and passengers. All was now excitement on
board. The hours of rest were passed by, and Than-Sing
overheard the robbers concerting their plans of attack, and
calculating the probable extent of the booty. When the
evening came, we were fastened down in our dungeon
more closely than ever.

It might have been about ten o'clock at night, when we
once more heard the frightful war-cries which startled us
from our sleep that fatal night on board the "Caldera."
These cries were followed by a dropping cannonade.
Two shots were then fired from our own junk, the vibra-
tion of which seemed to rend every timber around us.
More dead than alive, I vainly strove to still the beatings of
my heart, and dreaded every instant lest a ball should burst
in upon us. Four junks then surrounded the merchant-

vessel, which, taken by surprise, offered but a feeble resistance.

Amid the silence that ensued, Than-Sing contrived, with much difficulty, to raise the trap; for we had been a long time shut in, and the heat had become insufferable. Scarcely, however, had he succeeded, and looked out, than he drew precipitately back, and closed up the entrance. His terror and agitation alarmed me; but he refused to describe what he had seen. Some hours later, however, I learnt all that had taken place.

Having boarded and pillaged the merchant-junk, the pirates, it seemed, proceeded to interrogate the passengers. Several of these unfortunates unluckily confessed that they came from California, which was alone sufficient to expose them to every kind of ill-usage. In order to wring from them a full avowal of their riches, the pirates had put their victims to the torture. Bound by only one thumb and one toe, these wretched captives were suspended from the masts, and swung violently backwards and forwards. As if this were not sufficient suffering, their agonies were, from time to time, augmented by heavy blows, and their shrieks were inconceivably distressing. Although these scenes were not taking place on board our own junk, Than-Sing guessed but too plainly the species of torture which the barbarians had chosen to inflict.

Day broke, and the dreary silence which succeeded to the horrors of the night was only disturbed by the slow splashing of the waves, and the dipping oars of the rowers, who were transporting the booty in small boats from junk to junk.

CHAPTER VIII

Despair – I write the Date of my Captivity –
Benevolence of the Pirates – A Happy Meal – A
Steamer in Sight – Flight of the Pirates – Gratitude –
Hurrah! Hurrah! I am Saved!

WE had hoped that the day would, as usual,
bring us some little liberty and fresh air;
but the pirates were too busy to heed us. Absorbed
in the pursuit of gain, they were all day occupied
in negotiating the sale of their plunder, and for
that purpose received on board those traders
whose special line it is to buy up stolen goods.
Bathed in perspiration, racked with acute cramps,
and half stifled by the long-confined air, I suffered

horribly. My skin, too, was covered with a painful eruption, and I had become so weak that, although my companion strove to amuse and cheer me, I was no longer able to reply. By and bye, we heard the pirates counting their gold, and then the splashing oars that bore the purchasers away. This done, our jailers at length remembered our captivity, and opened the trap. It was time they did so; for we had lain there upwards of four-and-twenty hours! The delight which it was once more to breathe that fresh night-air, I shall remember to my dying day.

The next day was the 17th, and a glorious morning dawned. To our surprise, the pirates came at sunrise, and quite removed the trap. They seemed almost pleasant, and, when the hour of breakfast came, brought us not only an abundance of food, but even some wine. This liquor, which is extracted from rice, is as transparent as water, and by no means unpalatable. The flavour of it, indeed, is not unlike that of new Bordeaux.

The junk was now coasting beside an uninhabited shore, and the pirates, assured that we could not here be observed, left our cell uncovered throughout the day. They even suffered Than-Sing to remain for some time on deck, and behaved towards us with an amazing degree of good humour. The weather was so fine that I almost envied my companion, and longed to follow him in his walk. Not daring, however, to get out without permission, I ventured to stand up in my place, and look round at the land and the sea. Oh, how delicious seemed that sight! After having lived for seven long days in a dark and filthy den, I now beheld the broad bright ocean, the golden sunlight, the blue sky, and the verdant shore! Here and there, in the midst of trees and pastures, lay tiny white villages, dotting the coastline far away, like white flowers in the grass. The sight of this landscape intoxicated me. I fancied myself once more in sight of my own dear France, and wept as I have seldom wept before or since.

At this moment the pirate-chief passed by. I pointed to the land, and Than-Sing, who had been watching my emotion, hastened to explain that I was praying for life and liberty. Motioning to me to be calm, the chief then replied that he had long since despatched Captain Rooney in a junk to Macao; that Captain Rooney was empowered to treat there for our ransoms; and that he had expected yesterday to meet the junk on its return. Should five more days elapse, however, without further tidings, it was his intention, he said, to transfer us on board another vessel. This vague reply troubled us more than ever. Transferred to another junk, what might not be our fate? After all, the interpretation of the thing was plain enough. They were not disposed, somehow, to put us to death; but should they find it impossible to extort a ransom for our liberty, they would get rid of us to those who might not be so scrupulous. Even supposing that we had come across a steamer by the way, what had we to hope? Would not our captors sooner throw us overboard, than be taken in the fact of piracy and kidnapping on the high seas?

The captain now gave me leave to walk awhile on deck, and I gratefully availed myself of the permission. So happy was I in the enjoyment of light and liberty, that I forgot all my former tortures, and learnt to look upon these lawless men with feelings that were almost friendly. They were very busy this morning, bustling to and fro, chatting familiarly together, and dividing the spoil of the previous evening. I confess with shame that I scarcely remembered by what means they had wrung that spoil from their miserable victims, and could think only of my present freedom. It was not often that the pirates took any notice of me; but, strange to say, whenever they did look at me, it was with an expression of good-nature of which I should scarcely have supposed them capable.

"They like you," said Than-Sing, who had been talking with them. "They like you, because your face and eyes are gentle; and they say that they no longer wish any evil to happen to you."

It seemed incredible that these men should forego their native ferocity in my favour; but perhaps my patience and my weakness touched their hearts. On the other hand, I owed much, doubtless, to their cupidity. When I recall the length of my imprisonment, the character of my jailers, and all the circumstances of my capture, I can scarcely credit, even now, the evidences of my own memory.

Having been on deck for about two hours, I went back voluntarily to my cell. Long confinement had incapacitated me for any kind of exertion, and I fell down upon the floor, utterly wearied and exhausted. At the same time, I felt better than for many days past, and the weight at my heart was lightened.

Gazing languidly around the four dreary walls within which I had spent so many frightful hours, I observed an old book lying in one corner, covered with dust and dirt. I had seen it before, but had not till now the heart to take it up. It was a German work, and printed in German text. Ignorant as I was of the language, I turned the pages over with delight, for they reminded me of Europe and of home. At the end of the volume were some three or four blank leaves, still tolerably clean. "Oh," thought I, "had I but a pen, to record something of my story!" It then occurred to me that I had one hair-pin left, and that I might contrive to write with the point of it. My success surpassed my hopes, and the following words, thus traced upon the page, were sufficiently legible:

"I HAVE BEEN CAPTURED BY Chinese pirates, and am kept prisoner by them. I am a Frenchwoman, and was a passenger on board the 'Caldera'. This is my seventh day in the junk – 17th of October, 1854 – FANNY LOVIOT."

I then wrote the same thing in French upon another page, and, not content with this, took up a rusty nail that was lying near, and scratched my names, and the name of the "Caldera," upon the under-side of the framework into which the trap fitted. Each letter was an inch long, at the least, and no one searching the vessel could fail to see it. Alas! it was far from likely that any friendly eyes would ever behold it; and yet I loved to cherish every illusion that could help to veil the horrors of my present position. It was a dream, perhaps; but then it was a dream of France, and liberty!

As for the pirates, they kept passing backwards and forwards, and glancing down every now and then, to see what I was doing. They never guessed, however, that I was writing words which might, some day, hang every man among them!

Having recorded these three sentences, I lay down and rested. A thousand vague thoughts flitted through my mind, and hopes long fled began to dawn again. Profiting by my present privileges, I soon rose and went again on deck. The pirates were still friendly, and encouraged me to walk where they were at work; which I did, though not without misgivings. Some of them were busy launching a little boat, and Than-Sing explained to me that they were going to put off on an oyster-dredging expedition, which they presently did. It seemed that their first haul was fortunate, for they soon came back with the boat half full of enormous oysters, larger than any which I ever remember to have seen before.

The cook today was fully employed with his stewpans and braziers, and appeared to be giving himself airs of no little importance. A feast was evidently in course of preparation, and he well knew that on his skill depended the success or failure of the entertainment. First of all, he opened and shelled the oysters, and put them over the fire in a huge saucepan. He then fried a quantity of delicious little fishes, besides attending, every now and then, to a quarter of pork, which was browning before a fire close by. The sight of all these good things sharpened our appetites, and we asked each other if we had any chance of sharing the feast. When the hour of repast came round, Than-Sing and I went back to our dungeon, scarcely hoping to be remembered till the best of the dishes were eaten. How much, then, were we surprised, on finding the pirates assemble and seat themselves all round about our cell, while the cook, ladle in hand, went round, and helped the company to saucerfuls of smoking oysters. Of these, Than-Sing and I received as large a share as the rest, and although I was at first somewhat doubtful of the sauce in which they were floating, I soon came to the conclusion that I had seldom tasted anything more savoury. After the oysters came the pork, and after the pork, wine, tea, and fish fried in rice. We were liberally helped to all these dishes. Indeed, it seemed as if the pirates wished to show us how sociable they could be, and for this day, at least, we were treated less as prisoners than guests. They enjoyed the dinner immensely themselves, and more than once asked Than-Sing how I liked their cookery.

Towards the close of the feast, just as I was anticipating the comfort of a few hours' rest, a large merchant-junk came in sight to the leeward. Every man was on his feet in an instant, the remains of the dinner were cleared hastily away, the flags were hoisted to the mast-head, and the pirates, running eagerly hither and thither, prepared for fighting. Plunder was once again the order of the day, and we, crouched silently in our little den, awaited whatever might take place. The merchantman, however, made too much way for us, and the pursuit was presently relinquished. I was inexpressibly thankful that this comparatively happy day was not destined to end in bloodshed and pillage.

The merchantman was soon out of sight, and we were shortly overtaken by a flotilla of pirate-junks, the captains of which proceeded to make exchanges of merchandise and provisions. Amongst other things, our chief bought a quantity of live ducks. As night fell, the junks all dropped away, and we continued our solitary route.

At the hour of prayer we ventured out again, and walked on deck till nearly ten o'clock at night. The sky was calm and blue, and the stars shone. After my experience of the last few days, it seemed to me that I had never known any luxury so infinite. Tonight I observed that, instead of anchoring for several hours, as we had hitherto invariably done, we were sailing rapidly on, under press of canvass.

Going back to our dungeon, I lay as usual on the floor, and fell asleep thinking of the pleasant liberty which I had been suffered all day to enjoy. Waking from time to time, I heard the wind whistling through the cordage, and the rapid gliding of the waters as our keel ploughed onwards.

The next day was Wednesday, October 18th, 1854 – a heaven-sent day, never to be named unless with prayer and thankfulness! It might have been about four o'clock in the morning, when we were awakened from our sleep by the sound of hurrying feet and eager voices. After having sailed fast all the night, the junk was now riding at anchor, and the trap was closely fastened above our heads. I could not conceive what our captors were about, or why they should be thus active at so early an hour. The more I listened, the stranger it seemed. Having waited and wondered for some time, I tried to compose myself to sleep; but sleep would not come again, and, somehow or another, a strange restlessness possessed me. I turned to Than-Sing, who was awake and listening also, and asked him what he thought could be doing overhead? He laid his finger on his lip, and, bending breathlessly forward, paused for some moments before replying.

"Hush!" said he, at length. "They are going."

I could not imagine what he meant; but, just as I was about to question him further, he again motioned me to silence, and repeated, "They are going."

More puzzled than ever, I lay and looked at my companion, whose face expressed both joy and terror, and whose voice shook strangely.

"I tell you, they are going," said he. "It is a steamer in pursuit."

"A steamer!" I repeated, stupefied and incredulous. "A steamer!" I thought, for the moment, that my companion's brain was turned, and I was almost angry that he should dream of reawakening hopes which I had long since abandoned. Scarcely, however, had these thoughts crossed my mind, when he touched me on the shoulder, repeating, "It is a steamer! The pirates have seen a steamer, and they are escaping to the mountains."

I stared wildly in his face. My thoughts were all confusion. I dared not trust myself to take in the sense of his words.

"You are wrong," I said. "Would they lie at anchor if they were pursued?"

But he only pressed his face closely to the little port-hole, and replied, "Yes, it is a steamer! I see it! It is a steamer!"

My heart throbbed at these words, as if it would burst; and, looking out, I did indeed see a vessel at about two miles' distance. I say a vessel because there was no smoke visible. Alas! what if it were but a ship bound for Hong-Kong, Canton, or Macao? No such vessel would ever come to our succour, and what chance had we of being discovered on board a junk so similar to every other junk that sailed these seas? Notwithstanding my reasoning, however, I could not control my agitation, or keep away from the port-hole.

"Yes, yes," repeated Than-Sing, "they are going. They are flying from the steamer!"

"But it is not a steamer," said I. "There is no smoke. It is but a passing vessel, after all."

"I tell you that I am not mistaken. Steamer or no steamer, the pirates are fled! Listen how their voices die away."

I listened. A profound silence reigned around us, and I only heard a sound of murmuring voices, which became, every moment, more and more distant. I strove to raise the trap, but Than-Sing pulled me back. At that instant, a heavy footstep echoed overhead, and the trap was lifted from without. It was the ship's cook, who, with startled face and hurried gestures, looked in upon us.

"Fear nothing," said he. "It is a steamer! You are saved! It is a steamer!"

And with these words he also fled, and we were left alone. Quick as thought, I jumped up and sprang upon deck. A feverish strength possessed me, and I uttered cries of frantic joy. It was indeed true. We were alone, utterly alone, on board the junk, which, having anchored somewhat too close in shore, was left half stranded by the ebbing tide, and could not be pushed off. They had ventured here in search of fresh water, and it was not till daybreak that they found themselves in such close neighbourhood with the steamer. This latter, it seemed, was also lying at anchor, and had been partly hidden by a jutting tongue of land. Terrified, then, by the imminence of the danger, and finding it impossible to put off to sea, the pirates had preferred flight to fighting, and were, at this moment, abandoning their vessel. Having waded through the shallow water that lay between the ship's side and the land, they were now in the very act of climbing the steep precipices which here start, as it were, from the very verge of the sea. We could see them distinctly, and even the plunder with which they had loaded themselves.

No language can describe the emotion with which I beheld the flight of our enemies, and the near neighbourhood of those who would doubtless prove to be our friends. Incoherent words broke from my lips, and I paced to and fro with clasped hands and burning cheeks, eager for deliverance. In the meantime, those on board the steamer had not yet observed us, or put off a boat to our rescue. Seeing how near it lay, I would fain have tried to wade through the sea, like the pirates, and walk along the coast; but Than-Sing, who was cooler and wiser than I, would hear of no such attempt. "It is useless," said he. "They will be sure to come. Have patience, they will be sure to come."

His calmness exasperated me. I could not think why we need lose the precious moments, and I longed to go in search of the help that Heaven had sent us.

"Listen," said I. "Let us take the little boat, and put off to meet them. In an hour we shall have paddled up to the ship's side. Think, Oh think! what should we do if the pirates came back, and once more took us prisoners? Oh come, pray come!"

But Than-Sing was immoveable. "No, no," said he, with that phlegmatic gravity peculiar to his nation. "I tell you they will come to us. It is a steamer. They will come to us."

I grew desperate. It was the first disagreement that we had yet had, and I believed that he was wilfully sacrificing both our lives. Had I known how to swim, I believe I would have attempted the distance. As it was, I walked longingly round and round the small boat, and asked myself whether it were not possible to manage it alone. Had I strength enough to row or paddle two miles? Could I get it down into the sea? Might not the pirates even now return, and might not the steamer put off without having once perceived us? At the very moment when I was thus debating, I felt myself grasped by the arm, and found that Than-Sing had followed me to the after-deck.

"Look! look!" said he. "Do you see the three boats yonder?" I looked, and there indeed were three boats rounding a point of land, and making directly towards us. I tore off the chemise which I wore under my sailor's dress, and tied it to a piece of bamboo that was lying upon deck. I ran towards that side of the junk which lay nearest in their sight, and fixed my signal in a rift between the planking! There was now no fear, no doubt, no danger left! Ours was the only junk in sight, and the boats were already so near, that I could distinguish the blue jackets of the rowers. Than-Sing, standing beside me, crossed his hands upon his breast, and bowed his head in prayer. Dreading lest his Chinese dress should mislead our friends, I entreated him to keep out of sight; which he did, willingly.

All at once the rowers ceased to row, and sat in the boats with uplifted oars. Was it possible, after all, that they were about to give up, and go back to the steamer? Leaning breathlessly forward, I shaded my eyes with my hands, and knew not what to think. At this moment a volley of musketry was fired from all three boats, and a thick cloud of smoke was interposed between us. Taken by surprise, terrified, bewildered, I fell back, believing that it was their intention to attack the junk.

"Oh, my God!" I cried, falling upon my knees, "we shall be killed – killed by our deliverers!"

The thought that they might actually continue to fire, supposing the pirates to be still on board, inspired me with a sudden and desperate energy. "Let them shoot me face to face," thought I. "Come what may, I will make one effort more!" And with this I rushed to the prow, and showed myself again. I pulled off my cap – I waved it wildly to and fro – I tried to shout aloud, and immediately a prolonged "Hurrah!" broke from every lip, and told me that a crew of English sailors were our deliverers! They waved their hats in reply to my signal; then bent to their oars again, and cleft the waters as an arrow cleaves the air.

They had recognized me now, and we were saved at last!

CHAPTER IX

OVERWHELMED with joy, I staggered back, and fell, half-fainting, upon deck. By the time that I had recovered, the boats were within a yard or two of the junk. My strength was all gone now, and I wept profusely. I could not speak – I could not even think; and when our friends came climbing up the sides, and leaping on deck, I had no greeting to give them. They were chiefly soldiers and officers of the English marine service, and were accompanied by some blue-jackets and one or two sailor-officers. Captain Rooney was with them. He could scarcely contain his joy on seeing me again; and they all crowded round me with every mark of interest and good-will. As for poor Than-Sing, he was at first mistaken for a pirate, and had some half-dozen fists shaken in his face; but I ran and stood beside him, and Captain Rooney told them how he had saved us all, and how nobly he had behaved from first to last.

Finding that I was not too weak to be moved, the sailors then carried me down into one of the boats, and I left the junk for ever. While we were on our way, the officers explained to me that they had taken down the funnel of the steamer, in order to deceive and surprise the enemy. As to the volley of musketry which so alarmed me, they had fired only powder; hoping thereby to bring the pirates upon deck. Had I not gone forward again, and had I not waved my cap as I did, they would assuredly have fired next time with a deadlier purpose. As it was, the removal of the cap left my light hair visible, and Captain Rooney recognized me. When I first showed myself, they took me for a Chinese left in charge of the junk, and mistook my white signal for an alarm destined to recall the rest from shore. I also learnt that every one in Hong-Kong believed either that I had been killed, or that I was carried up into the country and sold. They, themselves, they said, had long since given up all hope of saving me.

When we were about half way between the junk and the steamer, the former was already in flames. As we drew nearer, we were greeted with loud cheers, which our rowers returned heartily. At the head of the steps by which we mounted upon deck, stood the captain, waiting to receive us. Seeing me, he came down part of the way, and supported me with his arm. He looked at me with as much amazement as pity, and, grateful as I was for this universal sympathy, I felt almost ashamed of the miserable condition in which I came amongst my deliverers. The deck was crowded with gentlemen, chiefly inhabitants of Hong-Kong and its neighbourhood, who had come out with the expedition from motives of curiosity and interest. Thankful to escape from every eye, I gladly retired to the cabin which had been prepared for my use. Here I found clothing and every necessary awaiting me, and hastened to make such a toilette as my weakness and weariness would allow. I looked at myself in the glass, and scarcely recognized my own features, so haggard were they, and so changed. My eyes were surrounded by livid circles, and my skin was blackened by the burning sea-winds. As for my hair, that was too hopelessly matted to be disentangled all at once;

so I was forced to leave it for awhile in its present disorder. While I was thus employed, the boats had started away again, to the attack of three or four pirate villages which lay close by in the creeks and coves of the coast.

When I was calmer, and had rested awhile, Captain Rooney told me all that had happened to himself and crew since we parted. Scarcely three hours had elapsed, he said, from the time of our departure, when another junk came up and took him on to Macao, leaving the crew with the wreck. Two hundred piastres was then agreed upon as the price of our ransom, and the pirates (confident of their own safety, since Than-Sing and I remained as hostages in the hands of their companions) sailed straight into port, and landed openly. Two of their number then followed Captain Rooney into the town, believing that he would immediately proceed to raise money among his friends. Captain Rooney, however, did no such thing, but presented himself at once before the governor, gave his two attendants into custody, and petitioned for immediate succours of men and arms, in order to rescue his crew, his passengers, and his ship, from the hands of the pirates. As Macao is a Portuguese colony, the governor could not undertake to furnish an expedition; but he granted Captain Rooney a military escort, and otherwise assisted him in removing his prisoners to Hong-Kong. Arrived at Hong-Kong, he went direct to M. Haskell, who was, as I have already said, our French vice-consul. It was midnight when Captain Rooney made his appearance at the consulate, and told his melancholy story. M. Haskell's trouble and amazement may easily be conceived. Late as it was, he took Captain Rooney with him, and went on board the "Sparta," then lying in harbour, under command of Admiral Sir William Hoste. Nothing could exceed the promptness and generosity with which this gallant officer hastened to place twenty-four marines at their immediate disposal; or the courtesy with which the Peninsular and Oriental Steam Packet Company lent the "Lady Mary Wood" for their conveyance. By six o'clock in the morning everything was in readiness, and they steamed out of harbour, taking the two prisoners with them, an interpreter skilled in the Chinese dialects, and several gentlemen who went for curiosity and excitement. During the greater part of the day they saw not a single sail. It almost seemed as if the pirates had anticipated pursuit, and purposely abandoned their accustomed haunts. Meeting, however, with some floating fragments of charred wood, they came upon the track of the "Caldera," and found but a few burnt fragments of her hull remaining. Struck with horror, they scarcely dared ask themselves what had been the fate of the crew, but made at once for some huts which lay at a considerable distance along the coast. These huts were inhabited by a few fishermen and their families; but they either were in league with the pirates, or really knew nothing of what had taken place, for no information could be got from them. The steamer then continued to coast close in shore, and landed at every village, on the chance of learning something definite. Just as they were disembarking at one of these little colonies, they were, to their surprise, greeted with a discharge of musketry, and found the inhabitants prepared to resist their landing. But it was information and not fighting of which the English were in search; so they hoisted a white flag, and sent one of the two Chinese prisoners to treat with his countrymen. In order to insure this fellow's fidelity, Captain Rooney pointed out to him a certain spot, beyond which he was to pass on no pretence whatever. At this point he was to stand and parley with the villagers, and if he but stepped beyond the assigned limit, he should be shot down like a dog. To these warnings he replied fairly enough, but no sooner found himself on shore, and at liberty, than he began running at full speed. "Stop!" cried the interpreter, just as the man neared the boundary which had been laid down for him. He stopped, hesitated, looked back as if measuring the distance, and then, possessed by the irresistible love of freedom, ran on again as fast as his legs would carry him. Scarcely, however, had he gone three yards, when the word was given to fire, and twenty balls were lodged simultaneously in his body. "He staggered," said Captain Rooney, "like a drunken man, dropped upon his knees, and fell never to rise again."

The villagers believing themselves attacked this time, replied by another volley, and a regular combat ensued. The English gained a rapid and easy victory, most of the Chinese fled after the second or third discharge, and only two or three of their number were killed after all. The marines and sailors then sacked and fired the village, and found a considerable quantity of merchandise belonging to the "Caldera," which they carried away in triumph. Having as yet heard nothing of us, and seeing but little likelihood of coming up just yet with any pirate-junks, the captain of the "Lady Mary Wood" prepared to return to Hong-Kong. Scarcely had they put the helm about, when they met a merchant-junk, with the whole of the crew of the "Caldera" on board. These poor fellows, it seemed, finding captain and passengers all taken from them, had made a last despairing attempt to escape in the same large boat which we vainly tried to navigate before. Although the sea and wind was, this time, more favourable to their efforts, they must have perished miserably, had they not been picked up by this merchant-junk, when distant but a few miles from the wreck. The "Lady Mary Wood" then took them on board, and a reward of 400 piastres was instantly paid over to the master of the junk, in acknowledgment of his humanity. The steamer then went back to Hong-Kong, without having yet discovered any traces of Than-Sing or myself.

Scarcely had the first expedition returned, when a second was organized, chiefly through the exertions and interest of M. Haskell. Another steamer, named the "Ann," set off in search of us on Tuesday, the 17th of October, 1854. Accident alone led the captain to steer in the direction of that very mountain under shelter of which our captors had chanced to anchor. The steamer and the junk, as we afterwards learnt, must have even reached the same spot much at the same time, and anchored within a couple of miles of each other, under cover of the darkness. It was not till morning that they perceived and rescued us in the order which I have already related; and the date of my deliverance was Wednesday, October 18th, 1854.

Listening to this account of all that had been done to save me, I quite broke down again, and had no words to speak my gratitude. Still more difficult was it to control my emotion when I read the following letter, which had been entrusted to Captain Rooney's care, in case of necessity:

"MADEMOISELLE, – Should this letter reach you, as I fervently hope it may, take some comfort, I entreat

you. If money alone be wanted for your deliverance, draw upon me for whatever ransom you may find necessary.

"G. HASKELL,

Vice-Consul of France at Hong-Kong."

Almost the whole day went by, and the three boats which had gone out in the morning were not yet returned. As dusk came on, the captain of the "Ann" became somewhat uneasy, and talked of weighing anchor and going in search of his men. Before he had time to do this, however, we were startled by the sight of a tremendous fire, at a distance of some three or four miles along the coast. A canopy of smoke rose high above the flames, and a red glare spread far and wide along the glassy surface of the sea. While we were yet looking, three dark objects emerged slowly from the farthest gloom, and came slowly on across the lighted waters. Then the moon rose, and we recognized the boats and their gallant crews. The men were greatly fatigued, but in high spirits, and full of the day's adventures. Having landed at a pirate village, they had fought a pitched battle with the inhabitants; put some to flight, and some to death;

discovered and carried off another large share of the cargo of the "Caldera;" and finally set fire to the village in four places at once. This time they brought back two prisoners. The sailors and marines vied with each other in describing their achievements, and seemed to delight in all the bloody details of the day. I heard one boasting of the number he had killed, and the hatred he bore towards these pagan pirates. "Hate the men as much as you like," said one of his companions, "but why be so cruel as to kill the women? I saw you shoot down a poor Chinese woman today, in cold blood!" "You are a fool!" replied the boaster, impatiently. "Wasn't she some pirate's mother?"

Next morning three boats, manned each by twenty hands, went out again – this time with the intention of rowing round the island, and surprising the pirates in the bay at the other side. The steamer followed them at some little distance, in case of need. We watched for a long time, and saw them round the cape and make towards the bay. At the very moment, however, when the next stroke would have carried them out of sight, we heard a sudden cannonade, and saw them pulling rapidly back. The bay, it seemed, was full of junks, to the number of forty or fifty, all armed and ready for combat; and the shores were lined with fortifications. Luckily the balls had but whistled above the heads of the rowers, and no harm was done. Deeming it useless to attack forces so numerous, the captain prudently weighed anchor, and put back for Hong-Kong. Having seventy miles of sea to traverse, we did not arrive till eight o'clock the next morning. The steamer was hung with ensigns taken from the enemy; and, just as we entered the Hong-Kong roads, our captain ran up a special flag, with the motto "All right," in token of my rescue.

Long before we landed, the news had spread throughout the city, and the quays were crowded. Numbers of boats put off and came to meet us, and every eye was searching for me among the passengers. Dressed as I still was, however, in male attire, it was not easy to distinguish me from the rest. I found myself overwhelmed with offers of hospitality. Mr. Walker, director of the Peninsular and Oriental Steam Packet Company, pressed me to stay with his wife and family; but, grateful as I was, I had made up my mind to take no steps till I had seen and thanked the vice-consul. Just as I was about to go in search of him, he came. He took both my hands in his, and looked at me with a countenance in which pity, joy, and benevolence were each struggling for the mastery.

"Come with me," said he simply. "I offer you shelter and protection in the name of France."

This one name went to my very heart, and I burst into a passion of tears. I blessed the Providence which had watched over me, and the dear fatherland which, even in these remote climes, opened its arms to receive me!

M. Haskell then led me to his own boat. A palanquin awaited me at the head of the landing-stairs, and in a few minutes more I crossed the threshold of a French home.

I spent twenty days at Hong-Kong, during which time I became the object of universal consideration. I was visited by every person of good standing in the city, and scarcely an European lady there but would have done anything to help and comfort me. Notwithstanding all this attention, I was forced to keep very quiet, and for a long time was too ill to receive any one. This immense joy, treading so closely on despair, proved too much for my strength, and an attack of brain fever followed. For several days and nights I raved of pirates, poignards, and fires. Nature triumphed at length; and, by the help of Heaven, I recovered quickly. Just at this time arrived a packet of letters from France and California; and I believe the home-news helped to cure me most of all. My only hope now lay with my friends and my country, and my only ambition was to return as soon as possible.

To lay in a stock of suitable clothing became one of the first cares of my convalescence; and I cannot describe the satisfaction with which I once more beheld myself in the attire of my sex. I may here remark, by way of paren-thesis, that in China the men are not only tailors, but dressmakers. All the dresses, linen, shoes, bonnets, and so forth, that I bought at Hong-Kong, were made by workmen.

Not many days before I left, I was gratified by a visit from Than-Sing. The good old Chinese was on his way to rejoin his wife and family at Canton, and came to bid me farewell. He was so richly dressed, that at first I scarcely knew him; but he told me that these clothes were all lent to him by a friend, since he, like myself, had been robbed of his entire wardrobe. We talked for a long time of all that we had suffered together, and parted with tears on both sides. As he left, he forced me to accept a richly embroidered handkerchief, as a *souvenir* of his friendship.

My departure was now fixed for the 11th of November, and the French government paid my passage to Marseilles, per Indian mail-packet. On the evening of the 10th, I received a visit from Captain Rooney and one of the lieutenants of the "Ann." This officer, after congratulating me on my improved health and appearance, presented me with a book, which I instantly recognized as that very German volume in which I had scratched, with a hair-pin, the records of my captivity. He had found it while searching the junk, and, chancing to take it up, opened the pages at the precise spot in which I had written. He wished, he said, to keep the book in memory of me and my strange adventures, and begged to be allowed to take it home with him to England. I was, of course, but too happy to grant so tri-fling a favour to one who had aided in my preservation.

As for Captain Rooney, he seemed sad and desponding enough. He felt, he said, as if some fatality hung over him; and, grown weary of a sea-life, now only longed to return to his home and his country. He wished me farewell for ever.

"If my prayers be granted," said he, "you will sail safely this time. Fear not – Providence watches over you."

CHAPTER X

ON the 11th of November, 1854, I was received on board the "Malta," government mail-packet. The vice-consul accompanied me on board, as if to assure me of his generous protection up to the very last moment of my stay, and I parted from him with feelings of such regret as I shall not attempt to put into words. Should this narrative ever meet his eyes, may he here read the earnest expression of my gratitude.

The line of route taken by the Indian mail-packets is certainly the most desirable for passengers. From Hong-Kong to Singapore is a journey of only seven days, and the steamer puts into port for twenty-four hours, which enables travellers to see something of the city. Singapore is chiefly inhabited by Chinese and Malays, and contains but few European families.

From Singapore to Penang takes but three days more, and here the steamer delays eight hours for the mails. These eight hours are, however, sufficient to enable a passer-by to judge of the infinite beauty of the place. It is verdant and luxuriant as a corner of paradise, and the most delicious fruits abound in every part.

Eight days after this, we touched at Point de Galle, in the island of Ceylon, where all the passengers were put on shore. The luggage was then transferred to another steamer, and the "Malta" continued her journey to Bombay. The number of travellers by this route is seldom large. We were but thirty-two, and consisted of English, Portuguese, and French. We all breakfasted together at a cottage-restaurateur's in the Jardin Canella, which is the public promenade of the place.

Embarking, towards evening, on board the "Bentinck," another steamer belonging to the same company, we started for Suez, and after ten days' travelling touched at Aden, for the purpose of taking in coals. It is a wretched spot – arid and desolate, and inhabited by a race of hideous and miserable human beings. Seven days on the Red Sea brought us to Suez, where I landed with real delight. We crossed the Isthmus in omnibuses, and our luggage was transported by a troop of camels. The camel-drivers were half of them blind, or nearly blind; for their eyes, during the transit across the desert, are perpetually attacked by myriads of flies.

Two refreshment-stations have been established along this route, for the benefit of travellers journeying between Cairo and Suez.

Cairo, as has been truly said many and many a time before, is a city taken from the pages of the "Thousand and One Nights." I shall not attempt to describe it here, for it has been described well and often, and I have nothing new to tell. I spent three days there, dreaming and wondering, strolling through bazaars and market-places, and visiting all that is most curious and surprising in the city and its neighbourhood. As for the Pyramids, although I saw them from afar in my passage down the Nile, I cannot say that I experienced any special delight or enthusiasm at the sight. Cairo, and Cairo alone, usurped all my admiration, and, far as I have travelled, and much as I have seen, I may truly assert that no spot I ever beheld could compare with it for novelty and magnificence.

From Cairo we proceeded by steamer down the Nile to Boulac, and at Boulac took the railway to Alexandria. Excepting a glimpse of the distant pyramids, and the sight of those quaint little mud-coloured Egyptian villages which lie scattered along the banks of the great river, this journey afforded no objects of interest by the way. At Alexandria I remained three days, waiting the arrival of my luggage. This city, unlike Cairo, is neither picturesque nor splendid. The bazaars are dirty, the population is scanty, and (being chiefly inhabited by Europeans) the oriental costume is but rarely seen. I visited the palace of the viceroy, Pompey's Pillar, and Cleopatra's Needle; but my heart was full of France and home, and I cared little for either modern palaces, or vestiges of a remote antiquity. How happy I was when I at length embarked on board the "Valetta," and knew that in six days more I should tread French ground! On the fourth day, we touched at Malta, but no one went on shore; and on the 26th of December, 1854, the "Valetta" cast anchor at Marseilles.

On the 30th I was in Paris, and read the following announcement in the columns of *La Presse*:

"Mademoiselle Fanny Loviot, who was taken prisoner not long since by pirates in the Chinese seas, has just returned to France in the 'Valetta,' via Marseilles."

Oh, the happiness of once more dwelling in the midst of those dear ones who had so often lamented me with tears, and believed me lost for ever! Oh, the delights of home, after the sufferings and dangers of a journey round the world! I went to seek my fortune, and found only misfortune. Still, with all their troubles, my weary wanderings had not been wholly profitless. I had beheld Nature, bountiful and beautiful Nature, under her most varied aspects; and if I had endured fatigue, privation, and even disease, I had, at least, lived that life of peril which hath its own peculiar charm for the imaginative and the young.

I have never yet regretted my journey, or its adventures. May the indulgent reader, who has followed me thus far in my narrative, as little regret the trouble of perusal!